To Rosaly,
on her 16th birthday

love from
    Mum & Dad,
              xx

QUOTABLE WOMEN

Quotable WOMEN

by
Carole McKenzie

MAINSTREAM
PUBLISHING

EDINBURGH AND LONDON

First published in Great Britain in 1992 by
MAINSTREAM PUBLISHING COMPANY
(EDINBURGH) LTD
7 Albany Street
Edinburgh EH1 3UG

ISBN 1 85158 494 3

A catalogue record for this book is available from the
British Library

Illustrations by Carolyn Ridsdale

Typeset in Sabon by Alphaset Graphics, Edinburgh
Printed in Great Britain by Mackays of Chatham plc

That's the point of quotations you know; one can use another's words to be insulting.

Amanda Cross, American writer

Acknowledgments

My special thanks go to Alison Payne who spent many hours helping to compile this collection:

She came, she saw, she conquered.

The only Aussie I know who not only can read the instructions in the computer users' manual, but can actually implement them.

Thanks also to Carolyn Ridsdale for her imaginative illustrations. Carolyn is particularly looking forward to illustrating the second book in the series – *Quotable Sex*.

And to Jim McKenzie who brought his daughter up to believe that everything is possible.

Preface

This is a book of quotations exclusively by women. It is a book that is long overdue, for while women are capable of great music, they rarely blow their own trumpets.

The need for a volume of this sort first struck me several years ago when I was writing a book called *Presenting for Women in Business*. I set out intending to introduce each chapter with a suitable quote by a woman, but when I turned to the general quotation literature I found that the few quotes by women were overwhelmed by sayings by men.

In any collection of quotations there is a need for accuracy – quotes are frequently attributed to people who never said them, or who said them in quite a different form or context to the one in which they are repeated. We take them up, edit, and often embellish them to fit our needs.

For ease of reference, the quotes that follow are arranged in alphabetical order.

They are sometimes amusing:

When a girl marries, she exchanges the attention of many men for the inattention of one.
Helen Rowland

Sometimes wicked:

Personally I like sex and I don't care what a man thinks of me as long as I get what I want from him – which is usually sex.
Valerie Perrine

Sometimes downright pornographic:

Like a drawing by a student in a life class, who was sitting at the back without his specs.
Victoria Wood

But always good sense:

I've never taken up with a congressman in my life . . .
I've never gone below the senate.
Barbara Howar

The astute observations and intuition of women has left a legacy of memorable lines from early centuries up to the present day. All are worthy because they express the thoughts, feelings, dreams and fears of women, irrespective of their social background or time in history.

ABILITY

Ability is sexless.
Christabel Pankhurst *(1880-1958), political leader of the militant suffragette campaign, and the daughter of Emmeline Pankhurst*

I'm not going to limit myself just because people won't accept the fact that I can do something else.
Dolly Parton, *American singer and actress*

When nothing is sure everything is possible.
Margaret Drabble, *British writer*

If you do things well, do them better. Be daring, be first, be different, be just.
Anita Roddick, *founder and managing director, Body Shop International*

As the newest Lady Turnpot descended into the kitchen wrapped only in her celery green dressing gown, her creamy bosom rising and falling like a temperamental soufflé, her tart mouth pursed in distaste, the sous-chef whispered to the scullery boy, 'I don't know what to make of her'.
Laurel Fortuner, *American writer, 1992 winner of the Bulwer-Lytton Prize (an annual contest to write the worst opening paragraph of an imaginary novel)*

Women are capable of great music but seldom blow their own trumpet.
Carole McKenzie

ACRONYMS

SINBADS
Women who are:– Single In Need of Blokes, in Absolutely Desperate State.

USWISOMWAGMOHOTM
United Single Women In Search Of Men Who Aren't Gay, Married, Or Hung-up On Their Mothers.

SCUM
Society for Cutting Up Men manifesto
Valerie Solanas, *American writer, book title, 1967*

ACTION

It is far easier to act under conditions of tyranny than to think.
Hannah Arendt (1906-75), German-American philosopher

ACTING

Acting is the most minor of gifts and not a very high-class way to earn a living. After all, Shirley Temple could do it at the age of four.
Katherine Hepburn

When I cry, do you want the tears to run all the way or shall I stop halfway down?
Margaret O'Brien (aged 6)

Acting is like painting pictures on bathroom tissues. Ten minutes later you throw them away and they're gone.
Shelley Winters, American actress

The stage is actor's country. You have to get your passport stamped every so often or they take away your citizenship.
Vanessa Redgrave

Acting is standing up naked and turning around very slowly.
Rosalind Russell

What acting means is that you've got to get out of your own skin.
Katherine Hepburn

Scratch an actor and you'll find an actress.
Dorothy Parker (1892-1967), American writer

I mean, the question actors most often get asked is how they can bear saying the same things over and over again night after night, but God knows the answer to that is, don't we all anyway, might as well get paid for it.
Elaine Dundy, The Dud Avocado, 1958

I was born at the age of twelve on a Metro-Goldwyn-Mayer lot.
Judy Garland (1922-69)

I'm glad you like my Catherine. I like her too. She ruled thirty million people and had three thousand lovers. I do the best I can in two hours.
Mae West (1892-1980), *American actress, speaking from the stage after her performance in* Catherine the Great

Dramatic art in her opinion is knowing how to fill a sweater.
Bette Davis *on Jayne Mansfield*

I just pretended I was a cartoon. I exaggerated every move. Every time I made a movement, I would think like a cartoon.
Kim Basinger, *on her role as a cartoon seductress*

All those actresses who turned the film away are stupid. I believe that if you have the right equipment and a point of view, that's a deadly combination.
Sharon Stone, *on her role in the film* Basic Instincts

If I quit the business tomorrow, I'd involve myself in working with people. That's why I love this profession.
Hannah Gordon, *actress*

I intend to keep entertaining people for as long as I can. I'm going to be like George Burns, an old trouper. And then, I hope, drop dead on the stage. If I rise and I look down and I see all that happening, I'll be happy.
Debbie Reynolds, *American film star*

The idea that acting is quintessentially 'feminine' carries with it a barely perceptible sneer, a suggestion that it is not the noblest or most dignified of professions. Acting is role-playing, role-playing is lying, and lying is a woman's game.
Molly Haskell, *American film critic and writer*

I do twenty minutes every time the refrigerator door opens and the light comes on.
Debbie Reynolds, *referring to her life in showbusiness*

I believe in being kind to others. I don't make life hard for myself. And I believe you have to learn something every day. When you stop, you die.
Evelyn Laye, *English actress and singer*

When you are my size, have dirty ashy blonde hair and look like me, you will never, never get to play glamorous roles. I'm just grateful my career has peaked with this success. Glory be! It's been wonderful. Generally, in this business, if you haven't made it by 40, you can forget it. We wrinklies can no longer be shoved in the back room and forgotten. That's the message I preach to the world . . . I make a good spokesperson. I'm a real bigmouth.
Estelle Getty, *American actress*

ADVERTISING

I have nothing to do with aspects of advertising; I can't even tell a Cinzano from a Martini. But I do trust the public to tell the difference between real life and advertisements, which is more than better-educated worthies seem willing to do.
Edwina Currie MP, *arguing in favour of advertising on the BBC and against the notion that advertising is bad for the public*

ADVICE

If you want a thing well done, get a couple of old broads to do it.
Bette Davis

I give myself sometimes admirable advice, but I am incapable of taking it.
Lady Mary Wortley Montagu *(1689-1762), British society hostess known for her witty and erudite letters. She introduced inoculation against smallpox into Britain*

Advice is what we ask for when we already know the answer but wish we didn't.
Erica Jong, *American writer and poet*

If I had to give young writers advice, I'd say don't listen to writers talking about writing.
Lillian Hellman *(1907-84), American playwright*

The strongest piece of advice I would give to any young woman is don't screw around and don't smoke.
Edwina Currie MP

Take the wife.
*Edwina Currie (then Junior Health Minister), advising
businessmen travelling abroad on how to avoid catching AIDS*

The way to a man's heart is through his stomach.
Fanny Fern (1811-72), American writer

Kill him.
Ivana Trump's advice to women deserted

Haste is the enemy of politeness.
Drusilla Beyfus

AFFAIRS

I knew about the affair . . . I told Paddy . . . 'look kiddo,
you've got to come clean or people will think that it's
something much worse'.
Jane Ashdown on her husband's much publicised affair

Baloney!
*Barbara Bush, wife of President George Bush, on the allegations
that her husband had had an affair*

I don't sleep with married men, but what I mean is that
I don't sleep with happily married men.
Britt Ekland, Swedish actress

If you are going to do something like my husband did,
you should at least have the decency to do it out of the
country, not next door. That's what any other man
would do.
*Lady Sarah Graham-Moon, after her husband, Sir Peter, began
an affair with a woman in the neighbouring village*

AGEING

Age – you just wake up one morning, and you got it.
Moms Mabley

Old age is not an illness, it is a timeless ascent.
As power diminishes, we grow towards the light.
May Sarton, Belgian-born American writer

If beauty is a letter of introduction – wrinkles are a
good résumé.
Mary Ellen Pickham

I refuse to admit that I'm more than fifty-two even if
that does make my sons illegitimate.
Nancy, Lady Astor (1879-1964), *the first woman MP to take a
seat in the House of Commons, 1919*

The years that a woman subtracts from her age are not
lost. They are added to other women's.
Diane de Poitiers (1499-1566), *mistress of King Henri II of
France*

A women is as young as her knees.
Mary Quant

Preparing for the worst is an activity I have taken up
since I turned thirty-five, and the worst actually began
to happen.
Delia Ephron

When a woman reaches twenty-six in America, she's on
the slide. It's downhill all the way from then on. It
doesn't give you a tremendous feeling of confidence and
well-being.
Lauren Bacall

The lovely thing about being forty is that you can
appreciate twenty-five-year-old men more.
Colleen McCullough, *writer*

I'd like to go on being thirty-five for a long time.
Margaret Thatcher (*at the age of fifty-four*)

The secret of staying young is to live honestly, eat
slowly and lie about your age.
Lucille Ball, *American actress*

I'm not interested in age. People who tell their age are
silly. You're as young as you feel.
Elizabeth Arden

Every age has a keyhole to which its eye is pasted.
Mary McCarthy, *American writer*, On the Contrary, 1962

Being seventy is not a sin.
Golda Meir (1898-1978), *Israeli leader*

I was born in 1962, true. And the room next to me was
1963.
Joan Rivers

You know, when I first went into the movies Lionel
Barrymore played my grandfather. Later he played my
father and finally he played my husband. If he had lived
I'm sure I would have played his mother. That's the
way it is in Hollywood. The men get younger and the
women get older.
Lillian Gish, *American actress*

Time and trouble will tame an advanced young woman,
but an advanced old woman is uncontrollable by any
earthly force.
Dorothy L. Sayers *(1893-1957), English writer*

Fifty-five years! I've sure come a long way from *Lassie*.
Elizabeth Taylor *on her birthday*

What is an adult? A child blown up by age.
Simone de Beauvoir *(1908-86), French writer, in* La Femme
Rompue

The older one grows the more one likes indecency.
Virginia Woolf in Monday or Tuesday

My forties are the best time I have ever gone through.
Elizabeth Taylor

All one's life as a young woman one is on show, a focus of attention, people notice you. You set yourself up to be noticed and admired. And then, not expecting it, you become middle-aged and anonymous. No one notices you. You achieve a wonderful freedom and it is a positive thing. You can move about unnoticed and invisible.
Doris Lessing, writer

The really frightening thing about middle age is the knowledge that you'll grow out of it.
Doris Day

When women pass thirty, they first forget their age; when forty, they forget that they ever remembered it.
Ninon de Lenclos (1615-1705), French society lady and wit

Being an old maid is like death by drowning, a really delightful sensation after you cease to struggle.
Edna Ferber (1887-1968), American writer

I have dedicated this celebration of life to the kid in me.
Elizabeth Taylor at her sixtieth birthday party at Disneyland

What happens to actresses after their forties? They get better but they stop working. There only seems to be room for a handful of women in middle age, but men in middle age can sustain careers all over the place.
Juliet Stevenson, English actress

I have always felt that a woman has the right to treat the subject of her age with ambiguity until, perhaps, she passes into the realm of over ninety. Then it is better she be candid with herself and with the world.
Helena Rubinstein (1862-1965), Polish-born cosmetics manufacturer, in My Life for Beauty

The closest seats always go first. For some reason, people want to see your fillings and wrinkles.
Cleo Laine, jazz singer, on her sell-out concerts at the Albert Hall

Get up dear, you're older than I am.
Queen Elizabeth, the Queen Mother, to Evelyn Laye (in her eighties) when she curtsied

There comes a time when you have to face facts about your face. Women whose age outstrips their bra size spend much time attempting to recapture their lost youth and I am no exception. But I have no desire to be young again. God forbid – all that fumbling, all that angst and acne. I just want to look younger – to find something that will stop the rot.
Nina Myskoff, *writer and columnist*

A I D S

It could be said that the AIDS pandemic is a classic own-goal scored by the human race against itself.
Princess Anne, *the Princess Royal*

She doesn't just go and shake hands with someone who's got AIDS to prove it's okay to shake hands; she actively goes to other countries to see how things are, and she marches around on foot to see for herself.
Audrey Slaughter, *ex-editor of* Vanity Fair, *on Princess Anne*

Every time you sleep with a boy you sleep with all his old girlfriends.
AIDS advertisement, 1987

A L I M O N Y

Billing minus cooing.
Mary Dorsey

Alimony is one way of compensating for those financial disabilities aggravated, or caused, by marriage: unequal educational opportunities; unequal employment opportunities; and unequal division of family responsibilities, with no compensation for the spouse who works in the home.
Susan C. Ross, *American lawyer and writer of* The Rights of Women

The high cost of leaving.
Anon

A M B I T I O N

When people inquire I always just state
'I have four nice children, and hope to have eight'.
Aline Murray Kilmer *(1888-1941), American poet*

We are all right in our place we are told – as controllers
of the household budget, educators of the minds of
children, folders of election addresses, but beware the
efforts of those who aspire to higher things.
Norah Willis *(1924-91), British feminist and President of the
Co-operative Congress, in a speech, 1983*

I have changed my ministers, but I have not changed my
measures; I am still for moderation and will govern by
it.
Queen Anne of England *(1665-1717) in a speech to the new
Tory Government*

A M E R I C A   A N D
A M E R I C A N S

In the United States there is more space where nobody
is than where anybody is. This is what makes America
what it is.
Gertrude Stein *(1874-1946), American writer*

When you get there [Oakland], there isn't any there
there.
Gertrude Stein

Natives who beat drums to drive off evil spirits are
objects of scorn to smart Americans who blow horns to
break up traffic jams.
Mary Ellen Kelly

The United States has the power to destroy the world,
but not the power to save it alone.
Margaret Mead *(1901-78), anthropologist and writer*

When an American heiress wants to buy a man, she at
once crosses the Atlantic.
Mary McCarthy, *American writer*

If there is any country on earth where the course of true
love may be expected to run smooth, it is America.
Harriet Martineau *(1802-76), British writer, in* Society in
America

Things on the whole are much faster in America; people don't stand for election, they run for office. If a person says he's sick, it doesn't mean regurgitating, it means ill. Mad means angry, not insane. Don't ask for the left-luggage; it's called the check room. A nice joint means a good pub, not roast meat.
Jessica Mitford, British writer

America has all that Russia has not. Russia has things America has not. Why will America not reach out a hand to Russia, as I have given my hand?
Isadora Duncan in a speech at the Symphony Hall, Boston in 1922 in support of Russia, following the 1917 revolution

The ladies have strange ways of adding to their charms. They powder themselves immoderately, face, neck and arms, with pulverised starch; the effect is indescribably disagreeable by day-light, and not very favourable at any time.
Frances Trollope (1780-1863)

I never saw an American man walk or stand well . . . They are nearly all hollow-chested and round-shouldered.
Frances Trollope

We grew up founding our dreams on the infinite promise of American advertising.
Zelda Fitzgerald (1900-48), wife of F. Scott Fitzgerald

In America you watch TV and think that's totally unreal, then you step outside and it's just the same.
Joan Armatrading

If you are going to America, bring your own food.
Fran Lebowitz, American journalist

Solitude is un-American.
Erica Jong

Once I was coming down a street in Beverly Hills and I saw a Cadillac about a block long, and out of the side window was a wonderfully slink mink, and an arm, and at the end of the arm was a hand in a white suede glove wrinkled at the wrist, and in the hand was a bagel with a bite out of it.
Dorothy Parker

Europeans used to say Americans were puritanical.
Then they discovered that we were not puritans. So
now they say we are obsessed with sex.
Mary McCarthy

ANGER

Anger as soon as fed is dead
'Tis starving makes it fat.
Emily Dickinson (1830-86), American poet

You don't pull ideas out of the air. What you've got to
do is find something that really makes you angry
because very often that's where there's a hole in the
market.
Anita Roddick

Anger makes dull men witty, but it keeps them poor.
Queen Elizabeth I (1533-1603)

My mother used to say 'he who angers you, conquers
you!' But my mother was a saint.
Elizabeth Kenny (1886-1952)

ANXIETY

A woman that loves to be at the window, is a bunch of
grapes on the highway.
English proverb

How often, while women and girls sit warm at a snug
fireside, their hearts and imagination are doomed to
divorce from the comfort surrounding their persons,
forced out by night to wander through dark ways, to
dare stress of weather, to contend with the snowblast,
to wait at lonely gates and stiles in the wildest storms,
watching and listening to see and hear the father, the
son, the husband coming home.
Charlotte Brontë

APPEARANCE

There are no ugly women, only lazy ones.
Helena Rubinstein

All women think they're ugly, even pretty women. A man who understood this could fuck more women than Don Giovanni. They all think their cunts are ugly . . . They all find fault with their figures . . . Even models and actresses, even the women you think are so beautiful that they have nothing to worry about, do worry all the time.
Erica Jong

In my own mind, I am still that fat brunette from Toledo and I always will be.
Gloria Steinem, American journalist and liberal feminist, one of the leading figures in the American women's movement in the 1960s

No one ever called me pretty when I was a little girl.
Marilyn Monroe

It's not what you'd call a figure, is it?
Twiggy

He has turned almost alarmingly blond – he's gone past platinum, he must be plutonium; his hair is co-ordinated with his teeth.
Pauline Kael, *American film critic, on Robert Redford*

Hair, in fact, is probably the bane of most women's lives.
Joan Collins

I looked like a lampshade on legs.
Julia Roberts *on her role as Tinkerbell in the film* Hook

Just look at the state of my nails. I've been wearing so much nail varnish over the last few weeks they've turned a sort of orangey colour.
Brigadier Gael Ramsey, *the first UK woman to command a garrison, and who is determined not to sacrifice her femininity*

If you try to mimic and ape men you're only going to be a crashing bore as a woman. I can live in combat kit and have no make-up on like the rest of the girls, but when I come back I like to think my nails are painted and I'm dressed for the occasion.
Brigadier Gael Ramsey

I used to iron my hair but now I love my curls.
Rabbi Julia Neuberger, *England's first female rabbi and the first in the world to have her own congregation*

Away from the cameras I always look dreadful, and so I go around dressed like a bag lady. At least that way I know I won't be recognised.
Michelle Pfeiffer, *American actress*

If people think I'm a dumb blonde, because of the way I look, then they're dumber than they think I am. If people think I'm not very deep because of my wigs and outfits, then they're not very deep.
Dolly Parton

The intoxication of rouge is an insidious vintage known to more girls than mere man can ever believe.
Dorothy Speare *(1898-1951), American writer and scenarist, in* Dancers in the Dark, *1922*

ARISTOCRACY

An aristocracy in a republic is like a chicken whose
head has been cut off: it may run about in a lively way,
but in fact it is dead.
Nancy Mitford, *British writer, in* Noblesse Oblige

ART

Art is the difference between seeing and just identifying.
Jean Mary Norman

All artists in whatever medium, in fact work largely
through the feminine side of their personalities. This is
because works of art are essentially formed and created
inside the mind of the maker, and are hardly at all
dependent on external circumstances.
Joan Rivers

In my experience, if you have to keep the lavatory door
shut by extending your left leg, it's modern architecture.
Nancy Banks-Smith, *British journalist and critic*

No artist is ahead of his time. He is his time. It is just
that the others are behind the time.
Martha Graham, *American dancer, choreographer, teacher and
director, considered the leading exponent of modern dance in the
USA*

If Michelangelo painted in Caesar's Palace, would that
make it any less art?
Cher

He is a delightful, kindly, friendly, simple little man,
and one would know him for a great man anywhere. At
the moment, he was extremely excited and overjoyed
because his mother-in-law had just died . . . and he was
looking forward to the funeral.
Dame Edith Sitwell *(1887-1964), British poet and writer, on
meeting Picasso*

Another unsettling element in modern art is that
common symptom of immaturity, the dread of doing
what has been done before.
Edith Wharton *(1862-1937), American novelist,* The Writing of
Fiction

A primitive artist is an amateur whose works sell.
Grandma Moses

As is the case in all branches of art, success depends in a very large measure upon individual initiative and exertion, and cannot be achieved except by dint of hard work.
Anna Pavlova (1881-1931), *Russian ballerina*

Art is the only thing that can go on mattering once it has stopped hurting.
Elizabeth Bowen (1899-1973), *Irish novelist,* The Heat of the Day

Any authentic work of art must start an argument between the artist and his audience.
Rebecca West (Cicely Isabel Fairfield; 1892-1983), *novelist and journalist,* The Court and the Castle

A photograph is not only an image (as a painting is an image). An interpretation of the real, it is also a trace, something directly stencilled off the real, like a footprint or a death mask.
Susan Sontag, American novelist and essayist

Sometimes I paint because it's the only way I can get out of a tizz. Wherever I am in the world I always stumble across an artist who takes me under his wing. There's this wonderful woman in Santa Barbara who taught me how to paint with vodka, kosher salt and clingfilm. I go to her house and get really crazy in the kitchen.
Jane Seymour, actress

Movies are so rarely great art that if we cannot appreciate the great trash we have very little reason to be interested in them.
Pauline Kael, American film critic

ATTITUDE

You've got to get up every morning with a smile on
    your face,
And show the world all the love in your heart.
Then people gonna treat you better.
You're gonna find, yes, you will,
That you're as beautiful as you feel.
Carole King

If you're too nice and charming you don't get anything done.
Barbara Cartland, romantic novelist

BACHELORS

A bachelor never quite gets over the idea that he is a thing of beauty and a boy forever.
Helen Rowland (1876-1950)

A bachelor has to have inspiration for making love to a woman, a married man needs only an excuse.
Helen Rowland

Never trust a husband too far, nor a bachelor too near.
Dorothy Parker

People always assume that bachelors are single by choice and spinsters because nobody asked them. It never enters their heads that poor bachelors might have worn the knees of their trousers out proposing to girls who rejected them or that a girl might deliberately stay unmarried because she didn't want to spend the rest of her life filling a man's stomach with food and washing his dirty shirts.
Jilly Cooper, Angels Rush In

BEAUTY

When I go to the beauty parlour, I always use the emergency entrance. Sometimes I just go for an estimate.
Phyllis Diller

God gave us our bodies and didn't expect us to go under the knife . . .
Rosemary Conley, author of the bestselling Hip and Thigh Diet, *on being asked whether she'd ever consider having plastic surgery*

Adornment is never anything except a reflection of the heart.
Coco Chanel

It's a good thing that beauty is only skin deep or I'd be rotten to the core.
Phyllis Diller

You can take no credit for beauty at sixteen. But if you are beautiful at sixty, it will be your soul's own doing.
Marie Stopes (1880-1958), Scottish birth-control campaigner who also wrote plays and verse as well as the bestselling manual Married Love, *1918*

I know cosmeticians would throw up their hands in horror but I don't believe you can block your pores with anything you put on your face, and I don't take my make-up off at night.
Dr Miriam Stoppard

I shall never get used to not being the most beautiful woman in the room. It was an intoxication to sweep in and know every man had turned his head. It kept me in form.
Lady Randolph Churchill

There is only one female comic who was beautiful as a little girl.
Joan Rivers

Is it too much to ask that women be spared the daily struggle for superhuman beauty in order to offer it to the caresses of a subhumanly ugly mate?
Germaine Greer

Beauty is altogether in the eye of the beholder.
Margaret Wolfe Hungerford (1855-97), Irish novelist

Taught from infancy that beauty is woman's sceptre, the mind shapes itself to the body, and roaming round its gilt cage, only seeks to adorn its prison.
Mary Wollstonecraft (1759-97), British feminist and radical intellectual, whose Vindication of the Rights of Women (1792) *demanded equal educational opportunities for women*

People may go on talking for ever of the jealousies of pretty women; but for real genuine, hard-working envy, there is nothing like an ugly woman with a taste for admiration.
Emily Eden (1797-1869), British-born Indian novelist

In high school and college my sister Mary was very popular with the boys, but I had braces in my teeth and got high marks.
Betty MacDonald (1908-58), American writer

That although artificial teeth are a great blessing, and although a suitable wig may be a charitable covering for a bald head, yet she is committing a sin against her personal appearance as well as against her self-respect if she dyes her hair.
Mary Scharlieb (1845-1930), British gynaecological surgeon, in The Seven Ages of Woman, *1915*

The two women gazed out of the slumped and sagging bodies that had accumulated around them.
Nadine Gordimer, South African writer and lecturer, and winner of the 1992 Nobel Prize for Literature, Vital Statistics, *1965*

There is nothing so lovely as to be beautiful. Beauty is a gift of God and we should cherish it as such.
Marie de Sévigné (1626-96), French writer

The beauty myth of the present is more insidious than any mystique of femininity yet; a century ago, Nora slammed the door of the doll's house: a generation ago, women turned their backs on the consumer heaven of the isolated multiapplianced home; but where women are trapped today, there is no door to slam. The contemporary ravages of the beauty backlash are destroying women physically and depleting us psychologically. If we are to free ourselves from the dead weight that has once again been made out of femaleness, it is not ballots of lobbyists or placards that women will need first; it is a new way to see.
Naomi Wolf, American writer, The Beauty Myth *1991*

I am lucky that I'm tall and blonde – that has encouraged the press to treat me well, and has given me a glamorous image beyond my swimming career.
Sharon Davies, *British record holder*

BEHAVIOUR

The less I behave like Whistler's mother the night before, the more I look like her the morning after.
Tallulah Bankhead *(1903-68), American actress*

The woman whose behaviour indicates that she will make a scene if she is told the truth asks to be deceived.
Elizabeth Jenkins

Funny really. When you look at the things that go on these days, my story reads like *Noddy*.
Diana Dors

If women are supposed to be less rational and more emotional at the beginning of our menstrual cycle when the female hormone is at its lowest level, then why isn't it logical to say that, in those few days, women behave the most like the way men behave all month long.
Gloria Steinem

It's the good girls who keep the diaries; the bad girls never have the time.
Tallulah Bankhead

My candle burns at both ends;
It will not last the night;
But Ah, my foes, and Oh my friends –
It gives a lovely light!
Edna St Vincent Millay *(1892-1950), American poet,* A Few Figs From Thistles

Any girl who was a lady would not even think of having such a good time that she did not remember to hang on to her jewellery.
Anita Loos *(1893-1981), American screenwriter,* Gentlemen Prefer Blondes

I'm proud that I was never vulgar. There's no way I'd need a tattoo or dress up in some surgical appliance to give folks a good night out.
Tina Turner, *referring to Cher*

As President Nixon says, presidents can do almost
anything, and President Nixon has done many things
that nobody would have thought of doing.
Golda Meir

He never does a proper thing without giving an
improper reason for it.
Lady Britomart in Major Barbara *by George Bernard Shaw*

B E L I E F

It doesn't pay well for what we believe in.
Lillian Hellman

We are apt to believe what the world believes about us.
George Eliot (Mary Ann Evans; 1819-80), British writer

You should always believe all you read in the
newspapers, as this makes them more interesting.
Dame Rose Macauley (1889-1958)

I stopped believing in Santa Claus when I was six.
Mother took me to see him in a department store and
he asked for my autograph.
Shirley Temple

I believe in the total depravity of inanimate things . . .
the elusiveness of soap, the knottiness of strings, the
transitory nature of buttons, the inclination of
suspenders to twist and of hooks to forsake their lawful
eyes and cleave only unto the hairs of their hapless
owner's head.
Katherine Ashley (1840-1916)

B I R T H   C O N T R O L

No woman can call herself free, who does not own and
control her body. No woman can call herself free until
she can choose consciously whether she will or will not
be a mother.
*Margaret Sanger (1883-1966), pioneer of American birth-control
movement*

We want far better reasons for having children than not
knowing how to prevent them.
Dora Russell (1894-1986), British campaigner and writer

The best contraceptive is a glass of cold water: not before or after, but instead.
Pakistani delegate at the International Planned Parenthood Conference

No, it is not because woman is lacking in responsibility, but because she has too much of the latter that she demands to know how to prevent conception.
Emma Goldman *(1869-1940),* The Social Aspects of Birth Control, *1916*

The contraceptive pill may reduce the importance of sex not only as a basis for the division of labour, but as a guideline in developing talents and interests.
Caroline Bird, *American writer,* Born Female, *1968*

BODY

Really that little dealybob is too far away from the hole. It should be built right in.
Loretta Lynn *on the female body*

Woman has ovaries, a uterus . . . it is often said that she thinks with her glands. Man superbly ignores the fact that his anatomy also includes glands, such as the testicles, and they secrete hormones.
Simone de Beauvoir

If I hadn't had them, I would have had some made.
Dolly Parton

My bust was visible under a negligée in one scene. Suddenly there were Barbra Streisand's breasts and I was worried that people might concentrate on my body instead of my acting.
Barbra Streisand *on seeing rushes of the sex scenes with Nick Nolte in the film* The Prince of Tides, *1991*

No, because it's true.
Montserrat Caballe, *opera singer, when asked if she gets upset when people comment on her weight. (She's been described as 'Monsterfat' and 'a sequined galleon under full sail'.)*

He must have had a magnificent build before his stomach went in for a career of its own.
Margaret Halsey, *American writer*

The body never lies.
Martha Graham, *American dancer and choreographer*

Fat is not about lack of self-control or will-power. Fat is about protection, sex nurturance, mothering, strength and assertion. Fat is a social disease.
Susie Orbach, *feminist psychotherapist*, Fat is a Feminist Issue, *1978*

Buttock fetishism is comparatively rare in our culture . . . Girls are often self-conscious about their behinds, draping themselves in long capes and tunics, but it is more often because they are too abundant in that region than otherwise.
Germaine Greer *in* The Female Eunuch

BOOKS

It takes the publishing industry so long to produce books it's no wonder so many are posthumous.
Teressa Skelton

Books, books, books. It was not that I read so much. I read and re-read the same ones. But all of them were necessary to me. Their presence, their smell, the letters of their titles, and the texture of their leather bindings.
Colette *(Sidonie-Gabrielle; 1873-1954), French writer*

I'm going to introduce a resolution to have the Postmaster General stop reading dirty books and deliver the mail.
Gale McGee

This novel is not to be tossed lightly aside, but to be hurled with great force.
Dorothy Parker

I am reading Henry James . . . and feel myself as one entombed in a block of smooth amber.
Virginia Woolf

The one thing I regret is that I will never have time to read all the books I want to read.
Françoise Sagan, *French novelist*

Having been unpopular in high school is not just cause for book publication.
Fran Lebowitz, *American journalist*

Perversity is the muse of modern literature.
Susan Sontag

We romantic writers are there to make people feel and not think. A historical romance is the only kind of book where chastity really counts.
Barbara Cartland

As artists they're rot, but as providers they're oil wells – they gush.
Dorothy Parker on lady novelists

Trivial personalities decomposing in the eternity of print.
Virginia Woolf, on Charlotte Brontë's Jane Eyre

Middlemarch, the magnificent book which with all its imperfections is one of the few English novels for grown-up people.
Virginia Woolf

Literature is strewn with the wreckage of men who have minded beyond reason the opinions of others.
Virginia Woolf in A Room of One's Own

I have only read one book in my life and that is *White Fang*. It's so frightfully good I've never bothered to read another.
Nancy Mitford (1904-73), British writer, The Pursuit of Love

Don't make me sound like a bookworm, because I'm not, but I'll read almost anything I can get my hands on, from women's magazines to Charles Dickens. I read because I enjoy it.
Lady Diana Spencer before her marriage to the Prince of Wales

Reading a book is like re-writing it for yourself . . . you bring to a novel, anything you read, all your experience of the world. You bring your history and you read it in your own terms.
Angela Carter (1940-92), British author

It was a book to kill time for those who liked it better dead.
Rose Macaulay (1889-1958)

Oh, I've got that one! Unfortunately my husband disapproves. He doesn't like me reading light novels.
Princess Diana, on seeing a Danielle Steele novel on a hospital patient's bedside table

B O R E D O M

Nothing is interesting if you're not interested.
Helen MacInness

Boredom results from a deficit of sensory
responsiveness to the external world.
Dr Estelle R. Ramey, *physiology professor, Georgetown
University*

B U S I N E S S

When I first approached the bank manager about a
£4,000 loan to start the first Body Shop in 1976, I
didn't have a clue about how to act. Then, twelve years
ago, there were no magazine articles telling you about
things like that. So I went dressed in my jeans and an
old Bob Dylan T-shirt, with my daughter Samantha on
my back in a papoose and Justine in the pushchair, and
started telling him about this great idea I'd had and how
wonderful it was going to be.
Anita Roddick, *founder and managing director, Body Shop
International*

I took a pair of old scissors. I cut the card into pieces
and sent it back to them in their prepaid envelope with
a letter protesting against a gross invasion of privacy.
Margaret Thatcher *on what she did upon receiving a credit card*

The display in the window has to be powerful. It must
shock you, and stop you in the street. It should be
controversial, it should be theatre.
Anita Roddick

I'm forcing more men into my company to get more
sexual tension into the business – because I love the
buzz and the sexuality of verbal foreplay.
Anita Roddick

Being Good is Good Business.
Anita Roddick

Women do have a lot to contribute to business. They've
got a lot of charm, charisma and common sense.
They're not so worried about their ego, they're not
afraid to say, 'I'm not sure how to do this'.
Debbie Moore, *founder of Pineapple Dance*

I often get invited to boardroom lunches as the token
woman; I find it tempting to say something outrageous.
Jennifer D'Abo, *former chairwoman, Ryman Ltd*

A lot of businesses are being started by women who
have been working for idiots for years. They know they
can do their boss's job, but they know they will never
be given it.
Jean Denton, *director of British Nuclear Fuels*

Businesswomen don't have to be aggressive when they
are dealing with men. It never works for them. If you're
good they can't argue with you.
Lynne Severn, *company secretary, Ford Holdings*

The notion that by succeeding academically or later, by
succeeding in any management you therefore destroy
your 'femininity' is the most pervasive threat against
women.
Lady Warnock, *Mistress of Girton College, Cambridge*

It was fun I'll admit, being the only woman at insurance
gatherings. But I had to be pretty careful not to convey
the impression of being a 'Typical Female'. I mean men
could afford to chatter on at times – or even be
frivolous – but I had to keep myself in check.
Eileen Kipling, *then Chief Underwriter, Equity and Law
Assurance*

'How high can a woman get in this bank?'
'Quite high enough.'
Conversation between **Jennifer D'Abo** *and banker*

It's hard to get to the top if you are a female in this country. The only way to do it is to run your own business. God help you if you ever want to be part of the petro-chemical industry or the banking world.
Anita Roddick

Business schools dampen entrepreneurship.
Anita Roddick

The role of the individual was to conform to the organisation. Now we believe organisations will have to conform more to the needs of the individual.
Anita Roddick

Marketing relies on pseudo-scientific language that proves nothing at all about the benefits of the product.
Bernadette Vallely, *director, Women's Environmental Network*

It's just called the Bible now – we dropped the word 'Holy' to give it more mass-market appeal.
Judith Young, *spokesperson, Hodder & Stoughton, Publishers*

I don't have any fucking duty to them at all. My only duty is to my company and to keep it alive in a way I think is right and honest.
Anita Roddick

Your readers are *my* shoplifters.
Betsy Bloomingdale, *Bloomingdale's department store, explaining to Rupert Murdoch why she would not advertise in his down-market* New York Post

I have always felt that our businessmen, if they had been left to themselves to make a religion, would have turned out something uncommonly like juju.
Mary Kingsley *(1862-1900), British ethnologist who made extensive explorations in W. Africa and wrote lively accounts of her findings*

We give customers a sense of theatre, a sense of the bizarre and we educate them.
Anita Roddick

Most managers never get out from behind their desks to see how things are done. If that means I'm thought of as something of a hippie, I don't care.
Anita Roddick

CANADA

If the national mental illness of the United States is megalomania, that of Canada is paranoid schizophrenia.
Margaret Atwood

It makes little difference; Canada is useful only to provide me with furs.
Madame de Pompadour (1721-64), *mistress of Louis XV, on the fall of Quebec*

CAREER

Journalism is the ability to meet the challenge of filling space.
Rebecca West

It is a horrible demoralising thing to be a lawyer. You look for such low motives in everyone and everything.
Katherine Tynan Hinkson (1861-1941), *Irish poet and novelist*

A science career for women is now almost as acceptable as being cheerleader.
Myra Barker

I thought of losing my virginity as a career move.
Madonna

I always wanted to be some kind of writer or newspaper reporter. But after college . . . I did other things.
Jacqueline Kennedy Onassis

The best careers advice to give to the young is: find out what you like doing best and get someone to pay you for doing it.
Katherine Whitehorn, British journalist

A caress is better than a career.
Elizabeth Marbury (1856-1933), *American playwright*, Careers for Women, *1933*

A career woman who has survived the hurdle of marriage and maternity encounters a new obstacle: the hostility of men.
Caroline Bird, American writer

The women's movement was very significant to my career. Without it people would have continued to assume that women could not be in high positions. It changed tradition, if it hasn't yet changed all the minds. I would not have been promoted so many times without that as a backdrop.
Joan Manley, *American publisher, in* Working Woman, *1979*

CHANGE

Out of every crisis comes the chance to be reborn, to reconceive ourselves as individuals, to choose the kind of change that will help us to grow and to fulfil ourselves more completely.
Nena O'Neill

The change of one simple behaviour can affect other behaviours and thus change many things.
Jean Baer

People change and forget to tell each other.
Lillian Hellman

Change your life today. Don't gamble on the future, act now, without delay.
Simone de Beauvoir

They take Paradise, put up a parking lot.
Joni Mitchell, *talking about change, in her song* Big Yellow Taxi, *1969*

I don't think he has changed that much. He still eyes a pretty lady – and why not? This is part of his magnetism. What has changed, I hope, is that he doesn't seem to have that urge to bed these lovely ladies. Now that's a major change.
Annette Bening, *on being asked what convinced her that marriage had changed Warren Beatty*

Nonsense, all of it, Sunnybrook Farm is now a parking lot; the petticoats are in the garbage can, where they belong in this modern world; and I *detest* censorship.
Shirley Temple Black, *American politician and former child star*

CHARACTER

Parents can only give good advice or put them on the right paths, but the final forming of a person's character lies in their own hands.
Anne Frank

Character contributes to beauty. It fortifies a woman as her youth fades.
Jacqueline Bisset

Character – the willingness to accept responsibility for one's own life – is the source from which self respect springs.
Joan Didion, American novelist and journalist

CHILDBIRTH

None of the fifteen legal men, comprising judge, senior and junior barristers and solicitors, had ever witnessed childbirth. Is it possible, the judge was to ask, for a woman to give birth standing up? Women have given birth under water, in aeroplanes, in comas, lying unnaturally flat on their backs in hospital beds and even after death, but this man wondered if they could do it standing up.
Nell McCafferty

The Queen of Scots is lighter of a fair son, and I am but barren stock.
Queen Elizabeth I, on the birth of the future King James VI of Scotland.

When a child enters the world through you, it alters everything on a psychic, psychological and purely practical level. You're just not free any more to do what you want to do. And it's not the same again, ever.
Jane Fonda

Dear Mary, We all knew you had it in you.
Dorothy Parker, in a telegram sent to a friend on the successful outcome of her pregnancy, 1915.

CHILDCARE

Childcare is the key to gaining women's support for the
Labour Party. Childcare is a bridging issue, and a vital
one that raises the question of whether women fighting
poverty are best helped only by welfare payments or by
being enabled to go to work.
Harriet Harman MP

By the end of this century 45 per cent of the working
population will be women. More than half of the
women with children under ten will be working and
will need pre-school or 'out of school' care (after school
and in the holidays). Childcare is now, therefore, not
just an important social issue, it is also a key to the
economy.
Harriet Harman MP

CHILDREN

An ugly baby is a very nasty object, and the prettiest is
frightful when undressed.
Queen Victoria

I blame Rousseau, myself. 'Man is born free', indeed.
Man is not born free, he is born attached to his mother
by a cord and is not capable of looking after himself for
at least seven years (seventy in some cases).
Katherine Whitehorn, British journalist

Remember that as a teenager you are at the last stage in
your life when you will be happy to hear that the phone
is for you.
Fran Lebowitz, American journalist

Sometimes when I look at my children I say to myself,
'Lilian, you should have stayed a virgin'.
Lilian Carter, mother of former American President Jimmy Carter

Never lend your car to anyone to whom you have given
birth.
Erma Bombeck, American journalist

My children are not royal. They just happen to have the
Queen for an aunt.
Princess Margaret

I knew I was an unwanted baby when I saw that my
bath toys were a toaster and a radio.
Joan Rivers

My obstetrician was so dumb that when I gave birth he
forgot to cut the cord. For a year that kid followed me
everywhere. It was like having a dog on a leash.
Joan Rivers

Thank God kids never mean well.
Lily Tomlin

The real menace in dealing with a five-year-old is that in
no time at all you begin to sound like a five-year-old.
Jean Kerr

The most ferocious animals are disarmed by caresses to
their young.
Fantine in Les Miserables *by Victor Hugo*

Oh, to be only half as wonderful as my child thought I
was when he was small, and only half as stupid as my
teenager now thinks I am.
Rebecca Richards

If you have never been hated by your child, you have
never been a parent.
Bette Davis

A child is fed with milk and praise.
Mary Lamb

The first thing I want to do is to see Eilish. I've missed
her so much. When I've got her in my arms, that's when
the celebrations can begin.
*Liz McColgan, Britain's first gold medallist at the World
Championships in Tokyo, on her nine-month-old baby*

I know I was cruel to other children because I
remember stuffing their nostrils with putty, and beating
a little boy with stinging nettles.
Vita Sackville-West, English writer

I've seen kids ride bicycles, run, play ball, set up camp,
swing, fight a war, swim and race for eight hours . . .
yet have to be driven to the garbage can.
Erma Bombeck in If Life is a Bowl of Cherries, What am I Doing
in the Pits?, *1978*

Let our children grow tall, and some taller than others if they have it in them to do so.
Margaret Thatcher in a speech during her 1975 American tour

Sons do not need you.
They are always out of your reach;
Walking strange waters.
Phyllis McGinley (1905-78), Canadian-born American writer of light verse, The Old Woman with Four Sons

If new-borns could remember and speak, they would emerge from the womb carrying tales as wondrous as Homer's.
Newsweek Magazine, *1982*

Children suck the mother when they are young and the father when they are old.
English Proverb

C H O I C E

Whenever I have a chance to choose between the two evils, I always like to try one I haven't tried before.
Mae West

COMFORT

It gives me a deep comforting sense that things seen are
temporal and things unseen are eternal.
Helen Keller *(1880-1968), American author. She became blind and
deaf through illness when only nineteen months old*

COMMUNICATION

Some people talk simply because they think sound is
more manageable than silence.
Margaret Halsey

The telephone is a good way to talk to people without
having to buy them a drink.
Fran Lebowitz

If you just say nothing there is no way they can make
you talk.
Twiggy

COMMUNISTS

Communists are people who fancied that they had an
unhappy childhood.
Gertrude Stein

CONSCIENCE

What I cannot live with may not bother another man's
conscience. The result is that conscience will stand
against conscience.
Hannah Arendt *(1906-75), German-American philosopher*

I cannot and will not cut my conscience to fit this year's
fashions.
Lillian Hellman, *American playwright, in a letter to the Chairman
of the House Committee on Un-American Activities.*

CONVERSATION

The real art of conversation is not only to say the right
thing in the right place but to leave unsaid the wrong
thing at the tempting moment.
Dorothy Nevill

COUNTRIES/PLACES

Latins are tenderly enthusiastic. In Brazil they throw
flowers at you. In Argentina they throw themselves.
Marlene Dietrich

When old settlers say 'one has to understand the
country', what they mean is 'you have to get used to
our ideas about the native'. They are saying, in effect,
'learn our ideas or otherwise get out; we don't want
you'.
Doris Lessing, referring specifically to South Africa, The Grass is
Singing

I told him I intended going to West Africa and he said,
'When you have made up your mind to go to West
Africa, the very best thing you can do is to get it
unmade again and go to Scotland instead; but if your
intelligence is not strong enough to do so, abstain from
exposing yourself to the direct rays of the sun, take four
grains of quinine every day for a fortnight before you
reach the rivers, and get yourself some introductions to
Wesleyans; they are the only people on the coast who
have got a hearse with feathers.'
Mary Kingsley, Travel in West Africa, *1897*

Africa, amongst the continents, will teach it to you; that
God and the Devil are one, the majesty coeternal, not
two uncreated but one uncreated, and the natives
neither confounded the persons nor divided the
substance.
Karen Blixen, Out of Africa, *1897*

The Atlantic seemed, as it still seems to me, a mere
obstacle to human intercourse, so opposite to the
Mediterranean's ballroom floor meant for
perambulation.
Freya Stark, Beyond Euphrates, *1951*

Nobody in England or America has any idea of the
intensity of the servant problem in the Southern
Hemisphere.
Dame Nellie Melba, Melodies and Memories, *1925*

Scotland is the country above all others that I have seen,
in which a man of imagination may carve out his own
pleasures; there are so many inhabited solitudes.
Dorothy Wordsworth, writing in her journal, August 1803

George wonders every day how we are allowed to keep this country a week.
Emily Eden, in a letter from India dated 21 June 1841

The pavement is the worst I ever walked on:– worse than Cologne: worse than my native city of Norwich.
Harriet Martineau describing Jerusalem in Eastern Life Past and Present, *1848*

Turks guard the door to keep Christians from fighting.
Lilian Leland in Travelling Alone – A Woman's Journey Around the World, *1890*

I can honestly say that if I was told at this moment that I was dying, not my first, not my second, but certainly my third thought would be that I should never see Italy again.
Mrs Henry Fawcett, Orient Line Guide, *1885*

It is a whole rock covered with very little earth.
Lady Mary Wortley Montagu describing Malta in a letter to the Abbé Conti, July 1718

November always seemed to me the Norway of the year.
Emily Dickinson

The French ladies may be said rather to plaster than to paint.
Eliza Fay

That little state like Hampstead Heath in the South of France.
Lady Docker on Monte Carlo

The people are unreal. The flowers are unreal, they don't smell. The fruit is unreal, it doesn't taste of anything. The whole place is a glaring, gaudy, nightmarish set, built upon the desert.
Ethel Barrymore (1879-1959), American actress, of Los Angeles

California is a place where a boom mentality and a sense of Chekhovian loss meet in uneasy suspension; in which the mind is troubled by some buried but ineradicable suspicion that things had better work here, because here, beneath that immense bleached sky, is where we run out of continent.
Joan Didion, American writer

COURAGE

Please know that I am quite aware of the hazards. I want to do it because I want to do it. Women must try to do things as men have tried. When they fail, their failure must be but a challenge to others.
Amelia Erhart (1898-1937), *in a letter to her husband before attempting to fly across the Pacific*

I've been through it all, baby. I'm Mother Courage.
Elizabeth Taylor

Courage comes from wanting to say it well; security comes from knowing you can say it well; confidence comes from having said it well.
Anon.

CREATIVITY

Creative minds always have been known to survive any kind of bad training.
Anna Freud

We are traditionally rather proud of ourselves for having slipped creative work in there between the domestic chores and obligations. I'm not sure we deserve such a big A-plus for all that.
Toni Morrison, *Pulitzer prize-winning American novelist*

DEATH

When I die, my epitaph should read 'She paid her bills'. That's the story of my private life.
Gloria Swanson

When I am dead, my dearest
Sing no sad songs for me.
Christina Rosetti (1830-94), *English poet*

I gave my life to learning how to live.
Now that I have organised it all . . . It is just about over.
Sandra Hochman

The fog is rising.
The last words of **Emily Dickinson** (1830-86)

Of course I am shocked by his death. But not nearly as shocked as when he walked out on me.
Sophie Levene, on hearing of Lord George Brown's demise.

Death must be an evil – and the gods agree; for why else would they live forever?
Sappho (sixth century BC)

Drink and dance and laugh and lie,
Love, the reeling midnight through,
For tomorrow we shall die!
(But, alas, we never do).
Dorothy Parker

Except taxes.
Elizabeth Bonaparte (1785-1879) in reply to someone who said that nothing was as sure as death

Am I dying or is this my birthday?
Nancy Astor, on seeing her children assembled round her sick bed during her last illness, 1964.

Death seems to provide the minds of the Anglo-Saxon race with a greater fund of innocent amusement than any other single subject . . . The tale must be about dead biddies or very wicked people, preferably both, before the tired businessman can feel really happy.
Dorothy L. Sayers

Whenever I prepare for a journey I prepare as for death. Should I never return, all is in order. This is what life has taught me.
Katherine Mansfield

If I had any decency, I'd be dead. Most of my friends are.
Dorothy Parker at the age of seventy

Death is my neighbour now.
Dame Edith Evans (1888-1976), English actress, a week before her death at the age of 88

Goddammit! He beat me to it.
Janis Joplin on hearing of Jimi Hendrix's death

In heaven they will bore you, in hell you will bore them.
Katherine Whitehorn

I have lost friends, some by death, others by sheer inability to cross the street.
Virginia Woolf, The Waves, *1931*

How could they tell?
Dorothy Parker's reaction to news of the death of American President Calvin Coolidge

Knight of the Crimean burial grounds, I suppose?
Florence Nightingale, referring to the KCB awarded to Dr John Hall, the British Chief of Medical Staff in the Crimea.

The bitterest tears shed over graves are for words left unsaid and deeds left undone.
Harriet Beecher Stowe (1811-96), American novelist, Little Foxes

Mine eyes have seen the glory of the coming of the
    Lord.
He is tramping out the vintage where the Grapes of
    Wrath are stored.
Julia Ward Howe (1819-1910), American writer, Battle Hymn of the American Republic

If they had said the sun and the moon was gone out of the heavens it could not have struck me with the idea of a more awful and dreary blank in the creation than the words: 'Byron is dead'.
Jane Welsh Carlyle (1801-66), in a letter to her husband Thomas, 1824

Grieve not that I die young. Is it not well to pass away ere life hath lost its brightness?
Lady Flora Hastings (1806-39), British poet

Human nature is so well disposed towards those who are in interesting situations, that a young person, who either marries or dies, is sure to be kindly spoken of.
Jane Austen (1775-1817), British novelist in Emma

I have nothing against undertakers personally. It's just that I wouldn't want one to bury my sister.
Jessica Mitford, British writer

I lingered round them, under that benign sky; watched the moths fluttering among the heath and harebells; listened to the soft wind breathing through the grass; and wondered how anyone could ever imagine unquiet slumbers for the sleepers in that quiet earth.
Emily Brontë, in Wuthering Heights

When we can't dream any longer we die.
Emma Goldman *(1869-1940), American anarchist*

DEATH – FAMOUS LAST WORDS

Do not grieve my friend – my dearest friend. I am ready to go – and John, it will not be long.
Abigail Adams *(1744-1818), wife of the second President of the USA*

Always! Always water for me.
Jane Addams *(1860-1935), American sociologist and feminist, on being asked if she would like a glass of water*

Smite my womb!
Agrippina, *mother of the Roman emperor Nero*

Is it not meningitis?
Louisa May Alcott *(1833-88), when asked about the nature of her illness*

Monsieur de Montaigu, consider what I owe to God, the favour he has shown to me, and the great indulgence for which I am beholden to him.
Queen Anne of Austria *(1601-66), wife of Louis XIII*

Use it for the good of my people.
Queen Anne of England *(1665-1714), on handing over the symbolic staff of the treasury to Lord Shrewsbury*

Nothing but death.
Jane Austen *(1775-1817), on being asked if she wanted anything (after months of ill health)*

Let me go, let me go.
Clara Barton *(1821-1912), founder of the American Red Cross*

The executioner is, I believe, very expert, and my neck is very slender.
Anne Boleyn *(1507-36), second wife of Henry VIII and mother of Queen Elizabeth I*

I always was beautiful.
Pauline Bonaparte *(1780-1825), sister of Napoleon*

Take courage, Charlotte, take courage.
Anne Brontë *(1820-49), aware that she was dying*

Oh I am not going to die am I? He will not separate us, we have been so happy.
Charlotte Brontë *(1816-55) to her husband. She had been married for only one year before she died*

If you will send for a doctor, I will see him now.
Emily Jane Brontë *(1818-48)*

Knowledge by suffering entereth and life is perfected by death.
Elizabeth Barrett Browning *(1806-1861), English poet who, when asked how she was feeling when dying, replied, 'Beautiful'*

I don't want it. I want to be left alone.
Marie Curie *(1867-1934), to a doctor coming to give her an injection*

Adieu, my friends, I go on to glory.
Isadora Duncan *(1878-1927)*

God is my life.
Mary Baker Eddy *(1821-1910), founder of the Christian Science movement*

Tell them I have great pain in the left side.
George Eliot *(1819-80)*

I pray you despatch me quickly. Will you take [the head] off before I lay me down?
Lady Jane Grey *(1537-54), Queen of England for nine days, to the executioner*

Napoleon . . . Elba . . . Marie Louise.
Marie Rose Josephine *(1763-1814), Empress of France, whose second husband, Napoleon, divorced her because she had not produced any children*

I am very forlorn at the present moment, and I wish I was at Malvern. Oh, don't I just!
Mrs Linn Linton *(1822-98), novelist*

My poor boy!
Dolly Madison *(1768-1849), wife of James Madison, fourth President of the USA*

Fie on the life of this world! Speak not to me of it any more.
Queen Margaret of Scotland *(1424-44), married at twelve years of age to the Dauphin Louis XI who hated and neglected her*

Yes, it is indeed frightful weather for a journey as long as the one before me.
Theresa Maria (1638-1683), *first wife of Louis XIV in reply to her son's comment on the rain*

Monsieur, I ask your pardon – I did not do it on purpose.
Queen Marie Antoinette of France (1755-93), *after stepping on the executioner's foot on the platform of the guillotine*

Get my swan costume ready.
Anna Pavlova

DEMOCRACY

Democracy means not I am as good as you are, but you are as good as I am.
Dorothy Parker

DESIRE

Want is the mistress of invention.
Susanna Centlivre (1667-1723)

DIAMONDS

No gold digging for me . . . I take diamonds! We may be off the gold standard someday.
Mae West

A diamond is the only kind of ice that keeps a girl warm.
Elizabeth Taylor

I prefer liberty to chains of diamonds.
Lady Mary Wortley Montagu (1689-1762), *English writer*

DIETS

Never eat more than you can lift.
Miss Piggy

Never eat after 6pm – you put on weight.
Kate O'Mara, writer

If you hear a great musician playing the piano, you don't feel a total failure because you can't do as well, do you? So why should a top model, whose job is being super-thin, make you feel inadequate? Food problems don't go away but you can stop giving yourself a bad time about them.
Victoria Wood

I'm also careful about what I eat. I'll eat a piece of chocolate cake for energy especially if I've been on the go all day.
Liza Minnelli

I feel the same about airplanes the way I feel about diets. It seems to me they are wonderful things for other people to go on.
Jean Kerr

Where do you go to get anorexia?
Shelley Winters

Give me a dozen such heart-breaks, if that would help me to lose a couple of pounds.
Colette

Those magazine dieting stories always have the testimonial of a woman who wore a dress that could slipcover New Jersey in one photo and thirty days later looked like a well-dressed thermometer.
Erma Bombeck

I've been on a constant diet for the last two decades. I've lost a total of 789 pounds. By all accounts I should be hanging from a charm bracelet.
Erma Bombeck

I've been on a diet for two weeks and all I've lost is two weeks.
Totie Fields (1930-78), *American entertainer*

. . . Unnecessary dieting is because everything from television to fashion ads has made it seem wicked to cast a shadow. This wild emaciated look appeals to some women, though not to many men, who are seldom seen pinning up a Vogue illustration in a machine shop.
Peg Bracken, *American humourist*

I stay in marvellous shape. I worry it off.
Nancy Reagan

First I lost my weight, then I lost my voice, and now I lost Onassis.
Maria Callas

Is she fat? Her favourite food is seconds.
Joan Rivers on Elizabeth Taylor, 1983

She's so fat, she's my two best friends. She wears stretch kaftans. She's got more chins than the Chinese telephone directory.
Joan Rivers

Oh no, great white whale.
Elizabeth Taylor, on her way to the refrigerator at the mid-point of her diet

Don't eat too many almonds, they add weight to the breasts.
Colette in Gigi

The right diet directs sexual energy into the parts that matter.
Barbara Cartland

My bathroom shelves have been quite streamlined over the past few years – since my healthy lifestyle has enabled me to throw out all the indigestion medicines I needed to calm my inflamed gall bladder. I don't keep any antacids now because our low-fat diet means my husband Mike and I never need them.
Rosemary Conley

DIFFERENCES BETWEEN MEN AND WOMEN

Men are generally more law-abiding than women. Women have the feeling that since they didn't make the rules, the rules have nothing to do with them.
Diane Johnson, American novelist

The main difference between men and women is that men are lunatics and women are idiots.
Rebecca West

Women are not men's equals in anything except
responsibility. We are not their inferiors either, or even
their superiors. We are quite simply a different race.
Phyllis McGinley, American poet

Perhaps men should think twice before making
widowhood our only path to power.
Gloria Steinem

God made men stronger but not necessarily more
intelligent. He gave women intuition and femininity.
And, used properly, that combination easily jumbles the
brain of any man I've ever met.
Farrah Fawcett, American actress

Mr Darwin . . . has failed to hold definitely before his
mind the principle that the difference of sex, whatever it
may consist in, must itself be subject to natural selection
and to evolution.
Antoinette Brown Blackwell (1825-1921), American feminist
writer, The Sexes Throughout Nature

I believe in the difference between men and women. In
fact, I embrace the difference.
Elizabeth Taylor

When a man confronts catastrophe on the road, he
looks in his purse – but a woman looks in her mirror.
May Sarton, Belgian-born American writer, in Mrs Stevens Hears
the Mermaids Singing

I don't think men and women were meant to live
together. They are totally different animals.
Diana Dors (1931-84), British actress

Women will normally respond to another woman
because they know what makes each other tick. A man
will not normally respond so quickly – you have to
show him you can maintain his confidence.
Brigadier Gael Ramsey

For him she is sex – absolute sex, no less. She is defined
and differentiated with reference to man and not he
with reference to her; she is the incidental, the
unessential as opposed to the essential. He is the
subject, he is the absolute – she is the other.
Simone de Beauvoir, (1908-86), French writer, in The Second Sex

When a man goes on a date he wonders if he is going to get lucky. A woman already knows.
Frederike Ryder

D I V O R C E

Getting divorced just because you don't love a man is almost as silly as getting married just because you do.
Zsa Zsa Gabor

Fission after fusion.
Rita Mae Brown, American author

Remarriage is an excellent test of just how amicable your divorce was.
Margo Kaufman

In our family we don't divorce our men – we bury them.
Ruth Gordon

You never really know a man until you've divorced him.
Zsa Zsa Gabor

Oh don't worry about Alan . . . Alan will always land on somebody's feet.
Dorothy Parker, on finalising her divorce from Alan Campbell

If divorce has increased one thousand per cent, don't blame the women's movement. Blame our obsolete sex roles on which our marriages are based.
Betty Friedan, American feminist. Her book The Feminine Mystique *(1963) was one of the most influential books for the women's movement*

It would be perfectly OK if men would graciously say, 'we've grown apart, let's be civilised about this, we are going to be friends.' But for so many women it's not like that . . . It's a very painful experience. I've got millions of letters from women like this. I recommend them not to surrender.
Ivana Trump of her divorce

Divorce is the sacrament of adultery.
French proverb

What scares me about divorce is that my children might put me in a home for unwed mothers.
Teressa Skelton

DRESS

I dress for women and undress for men.
Angie Dickinson, actress

You'd be surprised how much it costs to look this cheap.
Dolly Parton

I tend to wear outfits that match the walls.
Debra Winger, actress

My weakness is wearing too much leopard print.
Jackie Collins, British novelist

It is difficult to see why lace should be so expensive; it is mostly holes.
Mary Wilson Little

Elegance does not consist in putting on a new dress.
Coco Chanel

Brevity is the soul of lingerie.
Dorothy Parker

So I look ghastly, do I? I don't care, so long as I'm comfortable.
Katherine Hepburn

Oh yes, I like clothes – on other people. Well, somehow they seem to suffer a sea-change when they get on me. They look quite promising in the shop, and not entirely without hope when I get them back into my wardrobe. But then, when I put them on they tend to deteriorate with a very strange rapidity and one feels so sorry for them.
Joyce Grenfell

Fashion is architecture: it is a matter of proportions.
Coco Chanel

I haven't got the figure for jeans.
Margaret Thatcher

In England, if you are a duchess, you don't need to be
well dressed – it would be thought quite eccentric.
Nancy Mitford, Noblesse Oblige, 1956

Ever wish you were a man?
Never. I would hate not being able to dress up in
wonderful clothes and jewellery. I also think that
women are more creative than men. I'm very happy to
be a woman, thank you.
Sexiest men's clothes?
A black T-shirt and faded jeans, although everyone else
says a white T-shirt and jeans. I prefer men to look
casual, dinner suits are too stiff. My husband has a red
cotton sarong that he was given years ago. He always
wears it on holiday and when he's relaxing at home. He
looks wonderful in it.
Other career ambitions?
I'd love to explore other avenues of design, such as
swimwear, shoes and jewellery, but I have always
yearned to design the costumes for a really lavish film.
My clothes have been used in films and TV
programmes before, but I've never designed any specific
costumes. I saw the West End play *The Rehearsal*,
which Jasper Conran designed the costumes for, and
they were wonderful.
Edina Ronay, royal designer

Women dress alike all over the world: they dress to be
annoying to other women.
Elsa Schiaparelli, Italian fashion designer

Most women dress as if they had been a mouse in a
previous incarnation, or hope to be one in the next.
Dame Edith Sitwell (1887-1964), British poet and writer

It is puritanism, simply puritanism. It's all a kick against
society, against promiscuity, against drug-taking.
Laura Ashley, fashion designer, on her clothes.

The Republican Party couldn't make up their minds
whether I'd be mistaken for a trollop or for the Queen
of England. But silly as the request was, I stopped
wearing purple.
*Elizabeth Taylor (when Mrs John Warner), on being told by a
delegation from the Republican Party that she could no longer wear
purple*

A lady asked me why, on most occasions, I wore black.
'Are you in mourning?'
'Yes.'
'For whom are you in mourning?'
'For the World.'
Dame Edith Sitwell

All women's dresses are merely variations on the eternal
struggle between the admitted desire to dress and the
unadmitted desire to undress.
Lin Yutang (1895-1976), Chinese writer

You don't have to signal a social conscience by looking
like a frump. Lace knickers won't hasten the holocaust,
you can ban the bomb in a feather boa just as well as
without, and a mild interest in the length of hemlines
doesn't necessarily disqualify you from reading *Das
Kapital* and agreeing with every word.
Elizabeth Bibesco (1897-1945), British writer

Fashion is made to become unfashionable.
Coco Chanel

So fashion is born by small facts, trends, or even
politics, never by trying to make little pleats and
furbelows, by trinkets, by clothes easy to copy, or by
the shortening or lengthening of a skirt.
Elsa Schiaparelli

I only put clothes on so that I'm not naked when I go
out shopping.
Julia Roberts, American actress

What you wear is a problem. I like clothes and I love
shopping and that's a fatal combination.
Glenys Kinnock

It has always been an endless worry as to whether I
would ever have a whole garment and an unladdered
pair of stockings to wear. Poor old Ted pointed out to
me that his jacket was torn. My riposte was to pull out
my winter coat whose lining was falling apart for want
of a stitch, and tell him how embarrassed I was when
people at functions insisted on helping me into it.
Barbara Castle, British politician

Something warm, usually my husband.
Edwina Currie MP, on being asked what she wears in bed

I love American football gear. It's the tights I find sexy!
But I cannot imagine my husband dressed like that, he
looks best in comfortable sweaters and slacks.
Edwina Currie MP

DRINK

One more drink and I'll be under the host.
Dorothy Parker

The reason that I don't drink is that I want to know
when I am having a good time.
Nancy, Lady Astor (1879-1964)

He talked with more claret than clarity.
Susan Ertz (1894-1985), British novelist

Even though a number of people have tried, no one has
yet found a way to drink for a living.
Jean Kerr

Alcoholism isn't a spectator sport. Eventually the whole
family gets to play.
Joyce Rebeta-Burdett, The Cracker Factory, 1977

All along the line, physically, mentally, morally, alcohol
is a weakening and deadening force, and it is worth a
great deal to save women and girls from its influence.
Beatrice Potter Webb, British sociologist, writer and historian,
Health of Working Girls, 1917

EARTH

Only within the moment of time represented by the
present century has one species – man – acquired
significant power to alter the nature of the world.
*Rachel Carson (1907-64), American naturalist, aquatic biologist
and writer*

The most alarming of all man's assaults upon the
environment is the contamination of air, earth, rivers,
and sea . . . this pollution is for the most part
irrecoverable.
Rachel Carson

We won't have a society if we destroy the environment.
Margaret Mead (1907-78), American anthropologist

This could be such a beautiful world.
Rosalind Welcher

When the eagle of the north
flies with the condor of the south
The spirit of the land she will awaken.
Peruvian Inca Prophecy

ECONOMICS

Having a little inflation is like being a little pregnant –
inflation feeds on itself and quickly passes the 'little'
mark.
Dian Cohen

One of the soundest rules I try to remember when
making forecasts in the field of economics is that
whatever is to happen is happening already.
Sylvia Porter

Why does a slight tax increase cost you two hundred
dollars and a substantial tax cut save you thirty cents?
Peg Bracken

The trouble with being a breadwinner nowadays is that
the Government is in for such a big slice.
Mary McCoy

Inflation is the parent of unemployment and the unseen
robber of those who have saved.
Margaret Thatcher

EDUCATION

Men have had every advantage of women in telling
their own story. Education has been theirs in so much
higher a degree and the pen has been in their hands.
Jane Austen

A good education is usually harmful to a dancer. A
good calf is better than a good head.
Agnes de Mille, American dancer and writer

Education was almost always a matter of luck – usually
ill-luck in those distant days.
George Eliot

Prejudices, it is well known, are most difficult to eradicate from the heart whose soil has never been loosened or fertilised by education. They grow there, firm as weeds among stones.
Charlotte Brontë

To me education is a leading out of what is already there in the pupil's soul. To Miss Mackay it is a putting in of something that is not there, and that is not what I call education, I call it intrusion.
Muriel Spark, British novelist, *in* The Prime of Miss Jean Brodie

The right of education of the female sex, as it is in a manner everywhere neglected, so it ought to be generally lamented. Most in this depraved later age think a woman learned and wise enough if she can distinguish her husband's bed from another's.
Mrs Hannah Woolley (1623-75), *English governess, in* The Gentlewoman's Companion, *1675*

The cult of 'Arms and the Man' must reckon with a newer cult, that of 'Schools and the Woman'. Schools, which exalt brains above brawn, and women who exalt life-giving above life-taking, are natural allies of the present era.
Katherine Anthony (1877-1965), *American writer, in* Feminism in Germany and Scandinavia, *1915*

The most boring three years of one's life.
Margaret Forster, *writer, on her days at Somerville College*

Views expressed on the proposed co-ed move for an Oxford college:

I believe that women who want good academic qualification should be able to choose an all-women college. Men should similarly be able to go to all-men colleges.
Margaret Thatcher

Rather than going co-ed and giving up the ghost, the college should have led a major inquiry into the question of the number of women students and academics in colleges and insisted that the whole issue was reopened.
Shirley Williams

Somehow I think the presence of both sexes jammed so close together disturbs the monastic calm which is supposed to help study.
Iris Murdoch

E G O

The affair between Margot Asquith and Margot Asquith will live as one of the prettiest love stories in all literature.
Dorothy Parker *reviewing a book by Margot Asquith*

He was the cock who thought the sun had risen to hear him crow.
George Eliot

Egotism – usually just a case of mistaken nonentity.
Barbara Stanwyck, *American actress*

I will make you shorter by the head.
Queen Elizabeth I

I've been in *Who's Who* and I know what's what, but it's the first time I ever made the dictionary.
Mae West

If I ever felt inclined to be timid as I was going into a room full of people, I would say to myself, 'You're the cleverest member of one of the cleverest families in the cleverest class of the cleverest nation in the world, why should anyone be frightened?'
Beatrice Webb *(1858-1943), British economist and writer, in* Portraits From Memory

I don't mind how much my Ministers talk – as long as they do what I say.
Margaret Thatcher

I'm extraordinarily patient provided I get my own way in the end.
Margaret Thatcher

The male ego with few exceptions is elephantine to start with.
Bette Davis *in* The Lonely Life, 1962

With a head like yours I am surprised you don't get it circumcised.
Pamela Armstrong, *TV newscaster in a speech at the Cambridge Union*

EMOTIONS

I always wear boot polish on my eyelashes, because I am a very emotional person and it doesn't run when I cry.
Barbara Cartland

ENEMIES

Love your enemy – it will drive him nuts.
Eleanor Doan

I don't have a warm personal enemy left. They've all died off. I miss them terribly because they helped define me.
Clare Boothe Luce (1903-87), *American playwright, journalist and politician. She was editor of* Vanity Fair *in the 1930s and ambassador to Italy in the 1950s*

Enemies are so stimulating.
Katherine Hepburn

To have a good enemy, choose a friend; he knows where to strike.
Diane de Poitiers (1499-1566), *mistress of King Henri II of France*

ENERGY

Physical and mental energy come from feeling in control of your life, having real choices and being involved with others to find ways of organising for a change for the better.
Barbara Rogers

I think it's just fear of death. I can't bear to go to sleep. There's very little, you know, between an entrepreneur and a crazy person.
Anita Roddick

It is sad that my emotional dependence on the man I love should have killed so much of my energy and ability; there was certainly once a great deal of energy in me.
Sonya Tolstoy (1844-1919), *wife of Leo*

ENGLAND AND THE ENGLISH

Contrary to popular belief, Englishwomen do not wear tweed nightgowns.
Hermione Gingold

Those uncomfortable, padded lunatic asylums which are known euphemistically as the stately homes of England.
Virginia Woolf

The good manners of educated Englishmen . . . Such leaping to feet, such opening of doors, such lightning flourishes with matches and cigarettes – it's heroic. I never quite get over the feeling that someone has just said 'To the lifeboats!'
Margaret Halsey, *American writer*

I do love cricket – it's so very English.
Sarah Bernhardt (1844-1923), *French actress, on seeing a game of football*

The attitude of the English . . . toward English history reminds one a good deal of the attitude of a Hollywood director toward love.
Margaret Halsey *in| With Malice Toward Some*

Of course they have, or I wouldn't be sitting here talking to someone like you.
Barbara Cartland, *when asked in a radio interview whether she thought that British class barriers had broken down*

I know my heart to be entirely English.
Queen Anne (1665-1714), *drawing a contrast with her predecessor, the Dutchman William II, in a speech on the Opening of Parliament, 1702*

The Englishwoman is so refined she has no bosom and no behind.
Stevie Smith (1902-71), *British poet*

Living in England, provincial England, must be like being married to a stupid but exquisitely beautiful wife.
Margaret Halsey

The charm of Britain has always been the ease with which one can move into the middle class.
Margaret Thatcher

Even crushed against his brother in the tube the average Englishman pretends desperately that he is alone.
Germaine Greer

. . . A scene that is all English and stiff-upper-lip. Nothing is said that can be regretted. Nothing is said that can even be remembered.
Caroline A. Lejeune (1897-1973)

When it's three o'clock in New York it's still 1938 in London.
Bette Midler

ENVIRONMENT

I have always refused to wear cosmetics that have been tested on animals and to model fur coats throughout my career. Wearing a fur coat is unnecessary, absolutely disgusting and complete vanity. We have to stop women wanting them.
Twiggy

Working on the film *Gorillas in the Mist* was a very humbling experience for me. It made me realise how very vulnerable these animals are and I thought, 'If we can't protect them, how on earth are we going to protect ourselves?'
Sigourney Weaver, American actress

We have a great responsibility to protect lions and other endangered species. If we cock it up, there's no point making films such as *Born Free*. It would just be hypocritical.
Virginia McKenna, actress

Britain doesn't recycle enough.
Britt Ekland, actress

My house used to be like Blackpool illuminations with a light on in every room. But then I was put right in energy saving. My house will never be the same again.
Gloria Hunniford, *touring an energy-saving model home*

EQUAL OPPORTUNITIES

All the men on my staff can type.
Bella Abzug, *American politician*

Will you drive to the rescue?
Second World War poster, appealing to women

There was some opposition to women pilots to start with. People wrote in to *The Aeroplane* saying how wicked and contemptible it all was to employ them. The editor of the magazine wrote about women being a menace thinking they could cope with piloting a high-speed bomber, when some of them weren't intelligent enough to scrub a hospital floor decently. But I personally didn't come across any prejudice against women. We were soon treated equally and there was very little bias against us; eventually we got equal pay with men. After all, when there's a war on, you get on with your job.
Lettice Curtis, *British pilot during the Second World War,* Don't You Know There is a War On?

I am sorry that governments in all parts of the world have not seen fit to send more women as delegates, alternates or advisers to the assembly. I think it is in these positions that the women of every nation should work to see that equality exists.
Eleanor Roosevelt *(1884-1962), American writer and wife of Franklin D. Roosevelt*

It is of very doubtful value to enlist the gifts of a woman into fields that have been defined as male; it frightens the men, unsexes the women, and muffles and distorts the contribution women could make.
Margaret Mead *(1901-78) anthropologist and writer,* Male and Female, *1948*

There are very few jobs that actually require a penis or a vagina. All other jobs should be open to everybody.
Florynce R. Kennedy, *American lawyer and civil rights activist*

I earn my pay my own way as a great many women do today. Why should unmarried women be discriminated against – unmarried men are not.
Dinah Shore, *American singer and actress*

The feeling is that until men are comfortable working in some of these fields that are traditionally considered to be female . . . women end up doing two jobs, and the men are still doing just one.
Rosemary Brown, *Canadian politician*, Branching Out, *August 1975*

I don't believe in equal opportunity. I think it is terribly tiresome. The whole thing is absolutely terrible now because we've got vast unemployment. It is still a stigma for a man to be unemployed, and to be kept by a woman. It's not a stigma for a woman to be kept by a man.
Barbara Cartland

EQUALITY

We must have towns that accommodate different educational groups, different economic groups, different ethnic groups, towns where all can live in one place.
Margaret Mead

The real theatre of the sex war is the domestic hearth.
Germaine Greer

You're used. Used by what you are, eat, believe and who you sleep with. You can stop it. If you want equality, it has to start in bed. If he won't give it to you there, rip him off.
Jane Gallion

The only question left to be settled now is, are women persons?
Susan B. Anthony *(1820-1906), American writer and pioneering feminist who also worked for the anti-slavery movement*

I found nothing in the history of the Jews nor in the morals inculcated in the Pentateuch. I know of no other books that so fully teach subjection and degradation of women.
Elizabeth Cady Stanton *(1815-1902), American feminist who, together with Susan Anthony, founded the National Women's Suffrage Association*

A woman reading *Playboy* feels a little like a Jew reading a Nazi manual.
Gloria Steinem

They tell you that you bear none of the burdens of war. It is one of the great arguments brought against you when you ask for equal rights with men.
Droits des Femmes, *19th-century French suffragist journal*

Women who want to be equal to men lack ambition.
Anon

A black woman faces a three-fold disability in this country: she has to overcome the disadvantage of being black, the disadvantage of being a woman, and the disadvantage of her African cultural background in an essentially westernised environment.
Winnie Mandela

It's time people stood up and said women are getting too much of the action.
Tina Knight, businesswoman, who insists on no-pregnancy agreements with new recruits

A woman who thinks she is intelligent demands equal rights with men. A woman who is intelligent does not.
Colette (Sidonie-Gabrielle, 1873-1954), French novelist

The Bible and the church have been the greatest stumbling blocks in the way of women's emancipation.
Elizabeth Cady Stanton

Yes. It's partly our own fault. There was a heady time in the 1960s and 1970s when women – and I'm among them – thought that we really could have it all: a happy marriage, wonderful kids and a successful career. I now think there's always a price to be paid for everything and quite often women today find that this heady cocktail's a lot more painful than they thought it would be. Often the price you pay is sheer exhaustion. I don't know what you do about it – that's life. But hopefully men help out a bit more these days, so at least the burden at home can be halved.
Judy Finnigan, co-presenter of the TV programme This Morning

The prolonged slavery of women is the darkest page in human history.
Elizabeth Cady Stanton

Men their rights and nothing more; women their rights and nothing less.
Susan B. Anthony (1820-1906), American editor of The Revolution

Certain aspects of my philosophy have a distinct pre-feminist ring, but that's the way I was raised and the way I feel. Outside the workplace, anything less than equal pay is unacceptable.
Elizabeth Taylor

The IRS has stolen from me over the past 20 years because I am single. It is unconstitutional to impose a penalty tax of 40 per cent on me because I have no husband.
Vivien Kellems (1896-1975), American industrialist and feminist

It is ironic that the wife who made Britain great again, and who is the leader of the western world, has to get her husband to sign her tax form.
Jacqui Lait, on Margaret Thatcher, 1987

The best way to be supportive of other women is to get into situations in which you can change the rules – as a person, not as a woman.
Jean Denton, director of British Nuclear Fuels

Real progress has been made, the challenge is to hold on to it. Women believe themselves isolated but they are not. They have a joint purpose – never to accept artificial limitations impressed upon them solely through reason of their gender – and a joint investment in the future.
Caroline Norton (1808-77), British poet and campaigner for women's rights

It might be marvellous to be a man – then I could stop worrying about what's fair to women and just cheerfully assume I was superior, and that they had all been born to iron my shirts, better still, I could be an Irishman – then I would have all the privileges of being male without giving up the right to be wayward, temperamental and an appealing minority.
Katherine Whitehorn, journalist

It will be years – and not in my time – before a woman will lead the party or become Prime Minister.
Margaret Thatcher, when she was Minister for Health, 1974

Once a woman is made man's equal, she becomes his
superior.
Margaret Thatcher

Nothing could be more grotesquely unjust than a code
of morals, reinforced by laws, which relieves men from
responsibility for irregular sexual acts, and for the same
acts drives women to abortion, infanticide, prostitution
and self-destruction.
Suzanne Lafollette, American politician, feminist, writer and
editor

Foremost among the barriers to equality is the system
which ignores the mother's service to society in making
a home and rearing children. The mother is still the
unchartered servant of the future, who receives from
her husband, at *his* discretion, a share in *his* wages.
Katherine Anthony (1877-1965), American writer

Raising a family and doing housework are the common
tasks of a society, to be done equally by men and
women; along with this equality of shared necessity will
come equal pursuit of work, love, amusement, thought,
emotional independence and any other damn thing that
increases life and gives peace and pleasure.
Vivian Gornick, SCUM manifesto

The equal rights amendment is designed to establish in
our constitution the clear moral value judgment that all
Americans, women and men, stand equal under the law
. . . It will give woman's role in the home new status,
recognising that the homemaker's role in a marriage has
economic value.
Jill Ruckelshaus, American government official and lecturer

Those black males who try to hold women down are
expressing in sexist terms the same kind of expressions
in racist terms which they would deny.
Jacqueline Jackson, American writer

Once in a cabinet we had to deal with the fact that there
had been an outbreak of assaults on women at night.
One Minister suggested a curfew: women should stay
home after dark. I said, 'But it's the men who are
attacking the women. If there's to be a curfew, let the
men stay home, not the women.'
Golda Meir (1898-1978), Israeli Prime Minister

If the men in the room would only think how they would feel graduating with a 'Spinster of Arts' degree they would see how important this is.
Gloria Steinem, *referring to language reform in a speech at Yale University, 1981*

You can see exactly what your next step should be, but you realise there are all sorts of obstacles . . . a brick wall; a solid united front of male clubbability.
Valerie Hammond, *British management consultant*

At last, women have received their full citizenship papers, and yet . . . behind this celebration of the American woman's victory, behind the news, cheerfully and endlessly repeated, that the struggle for women's rights is won, another message flashes. You may be free and equal now, it says to women, but you have never been more miserable.
Susan Faludi, *American writer*, Backlash

EROTICISM

The residue of virility in the woman's organism is utilised by nature in order to eroticise her: otherwise the functioning of the maternal apparatus would wholly submerge her in the painful tasks of reproduction and motherhood.
Marie Bonaparte *(1882-1962) French psychoanalyst, sexologist and educator*

Women have been complaining to us for years that there is nothing like this on the market. They have a right to look at erotic pictures of beautiful men. They want explicit articles about sex. After all, men have been open and free about their sexuality for a long time.
Isabel Koprowski, *former editor of* Forum, *on the launch of* For Women

EXERCISE

Exercise, the last thing I want to do is go for the burn.
Meryl Streep

EXPERIENCE

Experience, a comb life gives you after you lose your hair.
Judith Stern

At every step the child should be allowed to meet the real experiences of life; the thorns should never be plucked from his roses.
Ellen Key (1849-1926), Swedish writer, The Century of the Child

It's but little good you'll do. A-watering the last year's crop.
George Eliot, in Adam Bede

FAMILY

No matter how many communes anybody invents, the family always creeps back.
Margaret Mead

As long as the family and the myth of the family . . . have not been destroyed, women will still be oppressed.
Simone de Beauvoir

FAME

I am so besotted by famous people . . . when I meet someone I really admire my mouth drops open and I can't say a word.
Judi Dench, British actress

FATHERS

We learn from experience. A man never wakes up his second baby just to see it smile.
Grace Williams

Freud is the father of psychoanalysis. It has no mother.
Germaine Greer in The Female Eunuch

The kind of man who thinks that helping with the dishes is beneath him will also think that helping with the baby is beneath him, and then he certainly is not going to be a very successful father.
Eleanor Roosevelt

It's shattering to be told that your father stinks.
Julie Nixon

FEAR

Nothing in life is to be feared. It is only to be understood.
Marie Curie

Fear has a smell, as love does.
Margaret Atwood

Everything is so dangerous that nothing is really very frightening.
Gertrude Stein

There are thousands of Sioux in this valley. I am not afraid of them. They think I am a crazy woman and never molest me . . . I guess I am the only human being they are afraid of.
Calamity Jane (Martha Jane Burke, 1852-1903), American frontierswoman

FEMINISM

If men could get pregnant, abortion would be a sacrament.
Florynce Kennedy

But if God wanted us to think with our wombs, why did he give us a brain?
Clare Boothe Luce

Social Science affirms that a woman's place in society marks the level of civilisation.
Elizabeth Cady Stanton

If particular care and attention is not paid to the ladies, we are determined to form a rebellion and will not hold ourselves bound by any laws in which we have no voice or representation.
Abigail Adams (1744-1818)

Take your secretary to lunch. He'll appreciate it.
Anon

Sometimes the best man for the job, isn't.
Anon

In the world we live in, feminism is a trivial cause.
Doris Lessing

Women's liberation is just a lot of foolishness. It's men who are discriminated against. They can't bear children. And no one's likely to do anything about that.
Golda Meir

Whatever women do they must do twice as well as men to be thought half as good. Luckily this is not difficult.
Charlotte Whitton, on becoming Mayor of Ottawa

I myself have never been able to find out precisely what feminism is: I only know that people call me a feminist whenever I express sentiments that differentiate me from a doormat.
Rebecca West

I would rather lie on a sofa than sweep beneath it.
Shirley Conran

Beware of a man who praises women's liberation; he is about to quit his job.
Erica Jong

Scratch most feminists and underneath there is a woman who longs to be a sex object. The difference is, that is not *all* she longs to be.
Betty Rollin

The major concrete achievement of the women's movement of the 1970s was the Dutch treat.
Nora Ephron

I'm furious about Women's Liberationists. They keep getting up on soapboxes and proclaiming that women are brighter than men. That's true, but it should be kept very quiet or it ruins the whole racket.
Anita Loos

Despite a lifetime of service to the cause of sexual liberation, I have never caught venereal disease, which makes me feel rather like an Arctic explorer who has never had frostbite.
Germaine Greer

Women are the only exploited group in history to have been idealized into powerlessness.
Erica Jong

No one should have to dance backward all their lives.
Jill Ruckelshaus, American government official and lecturer

When a woman behaves like a man, why can't she behave like a nice man?
Dame Edith Evans

I'm the most liberated woman in the world. Any woman can be liberated if she wants to be. First, she has to convince her husband.
Martha Mitchell

Never go to bed mad, stay up and fight.
Phyllis Diller

Adam was a rough draft.
Anon

A liberated woman is one who has sex before marriage and a job after.
Gloria Steinem

You can't be a feminist and a capitalist.
Ruth Wallsgrove, former member of the editorial collective and magazine Spare Rib

If you catch a man throw him back.
Women's liberation slogan in Australia, 1970s

I owe nothing to women's lib.
Margaret Thatcher

Of course there's no such thing as a totally objective person, except Almighty God, if she exists.
Antonia Fraser, British writer and historian

When you are born and they tell you 'what a pity that you are so clever, so intelligent, so beautiful but you are not a man', you are ashamed of your condition as a woman. I wanted to act like a man because the man was the master.
Melina Mercouri, Greek actress and political activist

The point of women's liberation is not to stand at the door of the male world, beating our fists, and crying 'Let me in, damn you, let me in!' The point is to walk away from the world and concentrate on creating a new woman.
Vivian Gornick, SCUM manifesto

I came very late to the women's mafia, which is our answer to the old boys' network. Theirs starts at school; we have to build ours subsequently.
Jean Denton

As though femininity is something you can lose the way you lose your pocket book – hmm, where in the world did I put my femininity?
Françoise Giroud, Swiss-born French politician, journalist and Minister for Women

I so much dislike the shape the women's movement has taken. There was an explosion of energy in the 1960s. I think it had a great deal of potential, but it has all been dissipated by talk. I do not begin to understand the terrible kind of masochism which is expressed by women identifying with this Madonna, who is a victim if I ever saw one, or Marilyn Monroe, and holding them up as some great feminist icon. Why should women, just when things are going much better for them, need to identify with failures?
Doris Lessing, novelist

I think the reason my generation bobbed and shingled their hair, flattened their bosoms and lowered their waists, was not that we wanted to be masculine, but that we didn't want to be emotional. War widows, many of them still wearing crêpe and widows' weeds in the Victorian tradition, had full bosoms, full skirts and fluffed-out hair. To shingle was to cut loose from the maternal pattern. It was an anti-sentiment symbol, not an anti-feminine one.
Barbara Cartland

In 1918 they bestowed the vote, just as they dropped about a few Dames and MBEs as a reward for our service in helping the destruction of our offspring . . . They gave the vote to the older women who were deemed less rebellious.
Dora Russell, British writer

To me the more important task of modern feminism is to accept and proclaim sex; to bury forever that lie that the body is a hindrance to the mind, and sex is a necessary evil to be endured for the perpetuation of our race.
Dora Russell

The whole idea of the feminist struggle being a peripheral kind of thing that you do in your spare time is something that has to be changed.
Rosemary Brown, *Jamaican-born Canadian politician*

But the whole point of liberation is that you get out. Restructure your life. Act by yourself.
Jane Fonda, *American actress, political activist, aerobics expert*

FIGURES

Ladies, here's a hint; if you're playing against a friend who has big boobs, bring her to the net and make her hit backhand volleys. That's the hardest shot for the well endowed.
Billie Jean King

It's impossible to be more flat-chested than I am.
Candice Bergen, *American actress*

FLIRTING

Flirt: a woman who thinks it's every man for herself.
Anon

FOOD

What I love about cooking is that after a hard day, there is something comforting about the fact that if you melt butter and add flour and then hot stock, *it will get thick*! It's a sure thing! It's a sure thing in a world where nothing is sure.
Nora Ephron

Before I was born my mother was in great agony of spirit and in a tragic situation. She could take no food except iced oysters and champagne. If people ask me when I began to dance, I reply, 'In my mother's womb, probably as a result of the oysters and champagne – the food of Aphrodite'.
Isadora Duncan

If I can't have too many truffles, I'll do without.
Colette

Everything you see I owe to spaghetti.
Sophia Loren

Cooking is like love. It should be entered into with
abandon or not at all.
Harriet Van Horne, American columnist

Large, naked, raw carrots are acceptable as food only to
those who live in hutches eagerly awaiting Easter.
Fran Lebowitz, American writer

Life is too short to stuff a mushroom.
Shirley Conran

Let them eat cake.
Queen Marie Antoinette of France (1755-93)

I have often seen the King consume four plates of
different soups, a whole pheasant, a partridge, a large
plate of salad, two big slices of ham, a dish of mutton in
garlic sauce, a plateful of pastries followed by fruit and
hard-boiled eggs. The King and Monsieur greatly liked
hard-boiled eggs.
Duchess of Orleans (1652-1722), sister-in-law to Louis XIV

F O O L S

Who's Virginia?
*Rose Kennedy, when asked why her daughter-in-law Joan lived in
Boston while her son Ted lived in Virginia*

In general, those who have nothing to say spend the
longest time saying it.
Amy Lovell

I believe that people would be alive today if there were
a death penalty.
Nancy Reagan

F O R G I V E N E S S

I shall be an autocrat: that's my trade. And the good
Lord will forgive me: that's his.
Empress Catherine the Great of Russia (1762-96)

F R E E D O M

To enjoy freedom we have to control ourselves.
Virginia Woolf

The freedom of the press works in such a way that there is little freedom from it.
Princess Grace of Monaco *(1928-82)*

F R I E N D S

You shall judge a man by his foes as well as by his friends.
Alice Brown

He's the kind of man who picks his friends – to pieces.
Mae West

Platonic friendship – the interval between the introduction and the first kiss.
Sophie Irene Loeb

Better bend than break.
Scottish proverb

I have always made a distinction between my friends and my confidants. I enjoy the conversation of the former but from the latter I hide nothing.
Edith Piaf, French singer

Business, you know, may bring money, but friendship hardly ever does.
Jane Austen in Emma

Every murderer is probably somebody's friend.
Agatha Christie *(1891-1976)*

Absence blots people out. We really have no absent friends.
Elizabeth Bowen *(1899-1973),* Irish novelist

God gives us our relatives. Thank God we can choose our friends.
Ethel Watts Mumford, American novelist, humorous writer

It's the friends you can call up at 4 a.m. that matter.
Marlene Dietrich *(1901-92)*

If we let our friend become cold and selfish and
exacting without a remonstrance, we are no true lover,
no true friend.
*Harriet Beecher Stowe (1811-96), American writer and social
critic*, Little Foxes, 1865

GENIUS

Genius is essentially creative; it bears the stamp of the
individual who possesses it.
Madame de Staël (1766-1817), French writer

The divine egotism that is genius.
Mary Webb (1881-1927), British author

Masterpieces are not single and solitary births, they are
the outcome of many years of thinking in common, of
thinking by the body of the people, so that the
experience of the masses is behind the single voice.
Virginia Woolf

Since when was genius found respectable?
Elizabeth Barrett Browning

GLAMOUR

Glamour is what makes a man ask for your telephone
number. But it is also what makes a woman ask for the
name of your dressmaker.
Lily Dache

My grandfather, Frank Lloyd Wright, wore a red sash
on his wedding night. *That* is glamour.
Anne Baxter

GOD

Sickness, sin and death, being inharmonious, do not
originate in God, nor belong to his Government.
Mary Baker Eddy, religious leader, Science and Health

The prayer that reforms the sinner and heals the sick is
an absolute faith that all things are possible to God – a
spiritual understanding of him, an unselfed love.
Mary Baker Eddy

So many Gods, so many creeds,
so many paths that wind and wind,
while just the art of being kind
is all the sad world needs.
Ella Wheeler Wilcox (1825-1921), *American poet,* The World's
Need

I have been into many of the ancient cathedrals – grand,
wonderful, mysterious. But I always leave them with a
feeling of indignation because of the generations of
human beings who have struggled in poverty to build
these altars to the unknown God.
Mary Baker Eddy

GOSSIP

If you haven't got anything nice to say about anybody,
come sit next to me.
Alice Roosevelt Longworth (1884-1980)

Men have always detested women's gossip because they
suspect the truth about their measurements are being
taken and compared.
Erica Jong, *American poet and writer*, Fear of Flying, 1973

GREED

Callous greed grows pious very fast.
Lillian Hellman

GROWING UP

Who's afraid of growing up? Who isn't? For if and
when we do begin the process of re-examining all that
we think and feel and stand for, in the effort to forge an
identity that is authentically ours and ours alone, we
run into our own resistance. There is a moment – an
immense and precarious moment – of such terror. And
in that moment most of us want to retreat as fast as
possible because to go forward means facing a truth we
have suspected all along: we stand alone.
Gael Sheehy, Passages

From birth to age 18, a girl needs good parents; from 18 to 36 she needs good looks; from 35 to 55 she needs a good personality; and from 55 on she needs cash.
Sophie Tucker (1847-1966)

You grow up the day you have the first real laugh – at yourself.
Ethel Barrymore

GUILT

A guilty conscience is the mother of invention.
Carolyn Wells

When a white man in Africa by accident looks into the eyes of a native and sees the human being (which it is his chief preoccupation to avoid), his sense of guilt, which he denies, fumes up in resentment and he brings down the whip.
Doris Lessing, The Grass is Singing

HABIT

Cocaine isn't habit-forming. I should know – I've been using it for years.
Tallulah Bankhead (1903-68)

Curious things, habits; people themselves never know they had them.
Agatha Christie

HAPPINESS

Happiness is a by-product of an effort to make someone else happy.
Grette Palmer

Happiness is not a state to arrive at, but a manner of travelling.
Margaret Lee Runbeck

When a small child . . . I thought that success spelled happiness. I was wrong. Happiness is like a butterfly which appears and delights us for one brief moment, but soon flits away.
Anna Pavlova (1881-1931), Russian ballerina

The happiest women, like the happiest nations, have no history.
George Eliot

H A T R E D

Misery generates hate; these sufferers hated the machines which they believed took their bread from them; they hated the buildings which contained these machines; they hated the manufacturers who owned those buildings.
Charlotte Brontë, *referring to the effect of the introduction of knitting frames into the mills in northern England*

H E A L T H

In a word, I am always busy, which is perhaps the chief reason why I am always well.
Elizabeth Cady Stanton

One cannot live well, love well or sleep well unless one has dined well.
Virginia Woolf

Nobody is healthy in London, nobody can be.
Jane Austen, Emma

The word 'spiritual' can make people cringe. Notebooks are shut and eyes turn to the skies.
The Princess of Wales *on the merits of spiritual healing*

H I S T O R Y

The defiance of established authority, religious and secular, social and political, as a worldwide phenomenon may well one day be accounted the outstanding event of the last decade.
Hannah Arendt *(1908-75), German-born American philosopher and historian*

H O L L Y W O O D

Living in Hollywood is like living in a lit cigar butt.
Phyllis Diller

Hollywood's a place where they'll pay you a thousand dollars for a kiss, and fifty cents for your soul.
Marilyn Monroe

No one ever went broke in Hollywood underestimating the intelligence of the public.
Elsa Maxwell

Hollywood – an emotional Detroit.
Lillian Gish

Hollywood is the only place in the world where an amicable divorce means each one gets fifty per cent of the publicity.
Lauren Bacall

If we have to kiss Hollywood goodbye, it may be with one of those tender, old-fashioned, seven-second kisses as exchanged between two people of the opposite sex with all their clothes on.
Anita Loos (1893-1981), American screenwriter

A deer in the body of a woman, living resentfully in the Hollywood zoo.
Clare Boothe Luce, American diplomat and writer, on Greta Garbo

H O M E

A man is so in the way in the house.
Mrs E. C. Gaskell, English novelist

The only really masterful noise a man ever makes in a house is the noise of his key, when he is still on the landing, fumbling for the lock.
Colette

Any woman who understands the problems of running a home will be nearer to understanding the problems of running a country.
Margaret Thatcher, May 1979

To the old saying that man built the house but woman made of it a 'home' might be added the modern supplement that woman accepted cooking as a chore but man has made of it a recreation.
Emily Post (1873-1960), American writer, Etiquette, 1922

A man's home may seem to be his castle on the outside; inside, it is more often his nursery.
Clare Boothe Luce

Go anywhere in England where there are natural, wholesome, contented and really nice English people; and what do you always find? That the stables are the real centre of the household.
Lady Utterwood *in George Bernard Shaw's* Heartbreak House

HOMOSEXUALITY

If homosexuality were the normal way God would have made Adam and Bruce.
Anita Bryant, *American anti-gay rights campaigner*

This is a celebration of individual freedom, not of homosexuality. No government has the right to tell its citizens when or whom to love. The only queer people are those who don't love anybody.
Rita Mae Brown, *American feminist writer, at the 'Gay Olympics', 1982*

People who have a low self esteem . . . have a tendency to cling to their own sex because it is less frightening.
Clara Thompson *(1893-1958), American physician, psychiatrist and educator*

HOUSEWORK

The best time for planning a book is while you're doing the dishes.
Agatha Christie

No one knows what her life expectancy is, but I have a horror of leaving this world, and not having anyone in the entire family know how to replace a toilet-tissue spindle.
Erma Bombeck

The idea of four babies, cooking, sewing and looking after the home suited me perfectly.
Laura Ashley, *fashion designer*

Housekeeping ain't no joke.
Louisa May Alcott, *in* Little Women

I hate housework! You make the beds, you do the dishes – and six months later you have to start all over again.
Joan Rivers

I am a marvellous housekeeper. Every time I leave a man I keep his house.
Zsa Zsa Gabor

It is not motherhood that keeps the housewife on her feet from dawn till dark; it is house service, not child service.
Charlotte Perkins Gilman (1860-1935), *American writer and lecturer*

I have too many fantasies to be a housewife – I guess I am a fantasy.
Marilyn Monroe

For a woman to get a rewarding sense of total creation by way of the multiple monotonous chores that are her daily lot would be as irrational as for an assembly-worker to rejoice that he had created an automobile because he tightened a bolt.
Edith Mendel Stern (1901-75), American writer

It was a strange stirring, a sense of dissatisfaction, a yearning that women suffered in the middle of the twentieth century in the United States. Each suburban wife struggled with it alone. As she made the beds, shopped for groceries, chauffeured cub scouts and brownies, lay beside her husband at night, she was afraid to ask even of herself the silent question, 'Is this all?'
Bette Friedan, American writer, The Feminine Mystique, 1963

You say being a housewife is the noblest call in the world . . . you remind me of those company executives who . . . praise the 'little guys' of their organisations in their speeches.
Françoise Parturier, French writer, Open Letter to Men, 1968

He thinks the washing, ironing and cleaning does itself (whilst I am at work) and when you say, 'who do you think just did all that washing?' the response is 'the washing machine'. What can you say?
Mrs Gillian Davies, on her husband's attitude to housework

H U M A N S

The fault is in us.
Hannah Arendt

No witchcraft, no enemy action had silenced the rebirth of new life in this stricken world. The people had done it themselves.
Rachel Carson

H U M O U R

He who laughs, lasts.
Mary Pettibone Poole

Personally, I can't see the appeal. Who would put their faith in a garment whose owner managed to get pregnant before she even reached for the top button.
Jaci Stephen, commenting on a piece of cloth allegedly belonging to the Virgin Mary's nightdress, for sale in Britain

Chaplin's genius was in comedy. He had no sense of humour.
Lita Grey, Charlie Chaplin's ex-wife

Humour is the first of the gifts to perish in a foreign tongue.
Virginia Woolf

H U S B A N D S

The reason husbands and wives do not understand each other is because they belong to different sexes.
Dorothy Dix (1870-1951), American journalist and writer

Husbands are like fire. They go out if unattended.
Zsa Zsa Gabor

A husband is what is left of a man after the nerve is extracted.
Helen Rowland

An archaeologist is the best husband any woman can have: the older she gets, the more interested he is in her.
Agatha Christie

If you cannot have your dear husband for a comfort and a delight, for a breadwinner and a cross-patch, for a sofa, chair or a hot water bottle, one can use him as a cross to be borne.
Stevie Smith

I think every woman is entitled to a middle husband she can forget.
Adela Rogers St John

I have three pets at home which answer the same purpose as a husband: I have a dog which growls every morning, a parrot which swears all afternoon and a cat that comes home late at night.
Marie Corelli

There is so little difference between husbands you might as well keep the first.
Adela Rogers St John

He was born to be a salesman. He would be an admirable representative of Rolls-Royce. But an ex-king cannot start selling motor-cars.
The Duchess of Windsor, referring to her husband

I've been asked to say a couple of words about my husband, Fang. How about 'short' and 'cheap'.
Phyllis Diller

The divine right of husbands, like the divine right of Kings it is hoped in this enlightened age, be contested without danger.
Mary Wollstonecraft, A Vindication of the Rights of Women

. . . A moody, broody Oriental. He was twenty years older than me but it might as well have been a hundred. He was really three hundred years behind me.
Zsa Zsa Gabor, on her first husband, Burham Belge

It is ridiculous to think you can spend your entire life with just one person. Three is about the right number. Yes, I imagine three husbands would do it.
Clare Boothe Luce

He is always dealing with beautiful women but it must be like being in a chocolate shop – after a while, you don't notice the goodies any more.
Barbara Taylor Bradford, English novelist, of her husband

My husbands have been very unlucky.
Lucrezia Borgia (1480-1519), to her father after the murder of her second husband

IDEALS

If a woman like Eva Perón with no ideals can get that far, think how far I can go with all the ideals that I have.
Margaret Thatcher

IDEAS

I am a powerful imager and if I want something to happen badly enough it usually does because I'm very tough with myself. I'm a good front person and I can make things happen. I have ideas which I can put into practice. Sting's ideas end up in songs – which pays the bills!!
Trudie Styler, *married to Sting*

IDENTITY

I began wearing hats as a young lawyer because it helped me to establish my professional identity. Before that, whenever I was at a meeting, someone would ask me to get the coffee – they assumed I was a secretary.
Bella Abzug

I was worried that by changing my name to Fowler I might lose my reputation for any expertise I might have acquired over the years.
Lady Fiona Fowler, *explaining why she uses her maiden name (Poole) at Westminster*

IMAGINATION

A lady's imagination is very rapid, it jumps from admiration to love, from love to matrimony in a moment.
Jane Austen

How to reconcile this world of fact with the bright world of my imagining? My darkness has been filled with the light of intelligence, and behold, the outer daylight world was stumbling and groping in social blindness.
Helen Keller, The Cry for Justice

Brain work is tiring; using one's imagination is not.
Enid Blyton (1897-1968)

IMPOSSIBILITIES

In the face of an obstacle which is impossible to overcome, stubbornness is stupid.
Simone de Beauvoir

IMPRESSIONS

When you were quite a little boy somebody ought to have said 'hush' just once.
Mrs Patrick Campbell (1865-1940, born Beatrice Stella Tanner), *British actress whose roles included Eliza in* Pygmalion, *written for her by G. B. Shaw, with whom she had an amusing correspondence*

Pale marmoreal Eliot was there last week, like a chapped office boy on a high stool, with a cold in his head.
Virginia Woolf on T. S. Eliot

All raw, uncooked, protesting.
Virginia Woolf on Aldous Huxley

Mr Lawrence looked like a plaster gnome in a stone toadstool in some suburban garden . . . he looked as if he had just returned from spending an uncomfortable night in a very dark cave.
Edith Sitwell on D. H. Lawrence

There are some people who leave impressions not so lasting as the imprint of an oar upon the water.
Kate Chopin, The Awakening

He looks as if he had been weaned on a pickle.
Alice Roosevelt Longworth, American hostess, referring to American President Calvin Coolidge

Lloyd George could not see a belt without hitting below it.
Margot Asquith

It is impossible to think of Howard Hughes without seeing the apparently bottomless gulf between what we say we want and what we do want, between what we officially admire and secretly desire, between, in the largest sense, the people we marry and the people we love. In a nation which increasingly appears to prize social virtues, Howard Hughes remains not merely anti-social but grandly, brilliantly, surpassingly asocial. He is the last private man, the dream we no longer admit.
Joan Didion

Smokers, male and female, inject and excuse idleness in their lives every time they light a cigarette.
Colette

The horrible little dwarf. He promised me a triumphal entry into Berlin. I'm afraid I laughed.
Marlene Dietrich on Adolf Hitler

The first time you meet Winston you see all his faults and the rest of your life you spend in discovering his virtues.
Lady Constance Lytton (1869-1923), British suffragette, referring to Winston Churchill

INDEPENDENCE

In too many negative ways women are subdued by their husbands. I'm not so dependent. I married at 30 when I knew who I was. I'm not Mrs Branagh. I was and always will be Emma Thompson.
Emma Thompson, actress

INFATUATION

Infatuation is when you think that he's as sexy as Robert Redford, as smart as Henry Kissinger, as noble as Ralph Nader, as funny as Woody Allen and as athletic as Jimmy Connors. Love is when you realise that he's as sexy as Woody Allen, as smart as Jimmy Connors, as funny as Ralph Nader, as athletic as Henry Kissinger and nothing like Robert Redford – but you'll take him anyway.
Judith Viorst, Redbook, 1975

INJUSTICE

Remember, no one can make you feel inferior without your consent.
Eleanor Roosevelt

Since when do you have to agree with people to defend them from injustice?
Lillian Hellman

When one has been threatened with a great injustice, one accepts a smaller as a favour.
Jane Welsh Carlyle (1801-66), wife of Thomas Carlyle

I don't deserve to be here. I had 116 bank accounts. I
never looked at them. It's so unfair.
Leona Helmsley, *American hotel queen, jailed for tax evasion*

INFIDELITY

. . . Adultery is a meanness and a stealing, a taking away
from someone what should be theirs, a great selfishness,
and surrounded and guarded by lies lest it should be
found out. And out of this meanness and this selfishness
and this lying flow love and joy and peace beyond
anything that can be imagined.
Dame Rose Macaulay *(1881-1958)*

Accursed from their birth they be
Who seek to find monogamy
Pursuing it from bed to bed –
I think they would be better dead.
Dorothy Parker

Benchley and I had an office in the old *Life Magazine*
that was so tiny, if it were an inch smaller it would have
been adultery.
Dorothy Parker

He's a 45-year-old man. I can't change the way he is.
Jennifer Flavin, *girlfriend of Sylvester Stallone, admitting she
knows that he cheats on her*

I prefer that word 'homemaker' because 'housewife'
always implies that there may a wife someplace else.
Bella Abzug, *American politician*

Of course I've known for years our marriage has been a
mockery. My body lying there night after night in the
wasted moonlight. I know now how the Taj Mahal
must feel.
Mrs Wicksteed *in Alan Bennett's* Habeas Corpus, *1973*

If fate had given me in youth a husband whom I could
have loved, I should have remained always true to him.
The trouble is that my heart would not willingly remain
one hour without love.
Catherine the Great *in a letter to Prince Potemkin, 1774*

INFORMATION

Everybody gets so much information all day long that
they lose their common sense.
Gertrude Stein

IRELAND AND THE IRISH

When anyone asks about the Irish character, I say look
at the trees. Maimed, stark and misshapen, but
ferociously tenacious. The Irish have got gab but are too
touchy to be humorous. Me too.
Edna O'Brien

In some parts of Ireland, the sleep which knows no
waking is always followed by the wake which knows
no sleeping.
Mary Wilson Little

She believed that Northern Ireland should be given back
to the Irish People, that it belonged to them. But it's just
those bastards who killed her.
Kate Meekings, *mother of 16-year-old Danielle Carter, one of the
IRA's bomb victims*

The Irish men are reckoned terrible heart stealers – but I
do not find them so very formidable.
Mary Wollstonecraft *in a letter to Everina Wollstonecraft, May
1787*

There is an Irish way of paying compliments as though
they were irresistible truths which makes what would
otherwise be an impertinence delightful.
Katherine Tynan Hinkson *(1861-1940), Irish poet and novelist*

JEALOUSY

Jealousy is the fear of losing the thing you love most.
It's very normal. Suspicion is the thing that's abnormal.
Jerry Hall

Jealousy is no more than feeling alone among smiling
enemies.
Elizabeth Bowen, The House in Paris

I think the only jealousy worth having is sexual jealousy. If I find something out, I go. I'm not a masochist. I don't hang around.
Jean Marsh, *English actress*

J O K E S

It's hard to be funny when you have to be clean.
Mae West

A difference of taste in jokes is a great strain on the affections.
George Eliot

K I S S I N G

In love there is always someone who kisses and one who offers the cheek.
French proverb

To a woman the first kiss is just the end of the beginning, but to a man it is the beginning of the end.
Helen Rowland

It takes a lot of experience for a girl to kiss like a beginner.
Ladies' Home Journal, *1948*

Wherever one wants to be kissed.
Coco Chanel, *when asked where one should wear perfume*

K N O W L E D G E

The more we know, the better we forgive: who 'ere feels deeply, feels for all who live.
Madame de Staël

Too clever is dumb.
German proverb

I'm as thick as a plank.
Princess Diana

Always be smarter than the people who hire you.
Lena Horne, *American singer*

Intellectuals can tell themselves anything, sell themselves any bill of goods, which is why they are so often patsies for the ruling classes in nineteenth-century France and England, or twentieth-century Russia and America.
Lillian Hellman

The good are so harsh to the clever,
The clever so rude to the good.
Elizabeth Wordsworth

Knowledge is power, if you know it about the right person.
Ethel Watts Mumford (1878-1940)

It is only middle-class people who, quite mistakenly, imagine that a lively pursuit of the latest in reading and painting will advance their status in the world.
Mary McCarthy

I've been called many things, but never an intellectual.
Tallulah Bankhead (1903-68), actress

LABELS

If lawyers are disbarred and clergymen defrocked, doesn't it follow that electricians can be delighted; musicians denoted; cowboys deranged; models deposed; tree surgeons debarked and dry cleaners depressed?
Victoria Ostman

You can't say 'The Noble and Gallant Lord is a silly old fool'. It wouldn't sound right.
Lady Phillips

No man, not even a doctor, ever gives any other definition of what a nurse should be than this – 'devoted and obedient'. This definition would do just as well for a porter. It might even do for a horse. It would not do for a policeman.
Florence Nightingale

Call me Madam.
Frances Perkins (1882-1965), American social worker and politician, deciding the term of address she would prefer when made the first woman to hold a Cabinet office in the USA

All the little hoops were set up for me to jump through, and when you jump, you get a reward – an image. But it's the image *they* supply . . . you become the perfect couple, or the faded English rose, or the wronged woman, or the rock and roll slut, or whatever. It has very little to do with real, manageable emotions.
Marianne Faithfull, *British singer and actress, referring to her relationship with Mick Jagger*

Chris is going to be His Excellency, but I don't know what I'll be called. Someone said to me the other day, 'Oh, you'll just be her indoors.'
Lavender Patten

LADY

A lady is someone who never shows her underwear unintentionally.
Lillian Day, *American writer*

LANGUAGE

Wonderful women! Have you ever thought how much we all, and women especially, owe to Shakespeare for his vindication of women in these fearless, high-spirited, resolute and intelligent heroines?
Ellen Terry *(1847-1928) British actress,* Four Lectures on Shakespeare: 'The Triumphant Women'

Language grows out of life, out of its needs and experiences . . . language and knowledge are indissolubly connected; they are inter-dependent. Good work in language presupposes and depends on a real knowledge of things.
Annie Sullivan *(1866-1936), American teacher of the handicapped*

LEADERS

A leader who doesn't hesitate before he sends his nation into battle is not fit to be a leader.
Golda Meir

LEARNING

To teach is to learn.
Japanese proverb

We could never learn to be brave and patient, if there were only joy in the world.
Helen Keller

Nothing would more effectively further the development of education than for all flogging pedagogues to learn to educate with the head instead of with the hand.
Ellen Key *(1849-1926), Swedish writer*

You've got to learn to love as you've got to learn to do other things and if you don't learn at the right time, you may never quite get your relations with human beings right. But in the meantime I don't think we can stop trying to get our prisons better until the world's perfect, or until all mothers are able to look after all children.
Marjory Fry *(1874-1958), worker for prison reform*

LESBIANISM

Lesbianism has always seemed to me an extremely inventive response to the shortage of men but otherwise not worth the trouble.
Nora Ephron, Heartburn, 1983

What's the point of being a lesbian if a woman is going to look and act like an imitation man?
Rita Mae Brown

Girls who put out are tramps. Girls who don't are ladies. This is, however, a rather archaic usage of the word. Should one of you boys happen upon a girl who doesn't put out, do not jump to the conclusion that you have found a lady. What you have probably found is a lesbian.
Fran Lebowitz, American journalist

My lesbianism is an act of Christian charity. All those women out there are praying for a man, and I'm giving them my share.
Rita Mae Brown

Refusal to make herself the object is not always what turns women to homosexuality; most lesbians, on the contrary, seek to cultivate the treasures of their femininity.
Simone de Beauvoir (1908-86), French writer and feminist

I have no doubt that lesbianism makes a woman virile and open in any sexual stimulation, and that she is more often than not a more adequate and lively partner in bed than a 'normal woman'.
Charlotte Wolff, Love Between Women, 1971

I never said I was a dyke even to a dyke because there wasn't a dyke in the land who thought she should be a dyke or even thought she was a dyke so how could we talk about it.
Jill Johnston, British-born American writer and feminist, Lesbian Nation, 1973

Lesbianism is not a matter of sexual preference but rather one of political choice which every woman must make if she is to become woman-identified and thereby end male supremacy.
N. Myron and **C. Burch**, Lesbianism and the Women's Movement, 1975

LIBERTY

Oppressed people are frequently very oppressive when first liberated . . . They know best two positions. Somebody's foot on their neck or their foot on somebody's neck.
Florynce Kennedy, American lawyer

Together hand in hand, with our matches and our [burning tyre] necklaces, we shall liberate this country.
Winnie Mandela

LIES

Lying is done with words and also with silence.
Adrienne Rich, American radical feminist poet, writer and critic

Sanity is a cosy lie.
Susan Sontag

Secretaries will never go to heaven. We spend half our time telling little white lies.
Gwen Cowan, *personal assistant to Sir Peter Parker*

Telling lies and showing off to get attention are the mistakes I made that I don't want my kids to make.
Jane Fonda

LIFE

The best-educated human being is the one who understands most about the life in which he is placed.
Helen Keller

What you get is a living – what you give is a life.
Lillian Gish

Life is my college. May I graduate well, and earn some honours.
Louise May Alcott

If I had my life to live again, I'd make the same mistakes, only sooner.
Tallulah Bankhead

What a wonderful life I've had; I only wish I'd realised it sooner.
Colette

People do not live nowadays. They get about 10 per cent out of life.
Isadora Duncan

Pigs and cows and chickens and people are all competing for grain.
Margaret Mead

Better to enjoy and suffer than to sit around with folded arms. You know the only true prayer? Please God, lead me into temptation.
Jennie Lee, *British politician*, My Life With Nye

We're all in this alone.
Lily Tomlin, *American comedy actress*

Life's what's important. Walking, houses, family, birth and pain and joy. Acting's just waiting for the custard pie.
Katherine Hepburn

Books succeed and lives fail.
Elizabeth Barrett Browning

Some say life is the thing, but I prefer reading.
Ruth Rendell

I've looked at life from both sides now
From win and lose and still somehow
It's life's illusions I recall
I really don't know life at all.
Joni Mitchell, Canadian singer/songwriter, Both Sides Now

The first rule in Opera is the first rule in life; see to
everything yourself.
Nellie Melba (1861-1931), Australian soprano, Melodies and
Memories

I have learned to live each day as it comes, and not to
borrow trouble by dreading tomorrow. It is the dark
menace of the future that makes cowards of us.
*Dorothy Dix (Elizabeth Meriwether Gilmer, 1861-1951),
American journalist and writer*

The trouble with the rat race is that even if you win,
you're still a rat.
Lily Tomlin

The most exhausting thing in life is being insincere.
That is why so much social life is exhausting.
Anne Morrow Lindbergh

Life is nothing but a series of crosses for us mothers.
Colette

One never notices what has been done; one can only see
what remains to be done.
Marie Curie (1867-1934)

LIVING

It is only possible to live happily ever after on a day-to-
day basis.
Margaret Bonnano

Millions long for immortality who do not know what
to do with themselves on a rainy Sunday afternoon.
Susan Ertz, British writer

Only when one is no longer afraid to die is one no longer afraid at all. And only when we are no longer afraid, do we begin to live in every experience, painful or joyous, to live in gratitude for every moment, to live abundantly.
Dorothy Thompson

Civilisation is a method of living, an attitude of equal respect for all men.
Jane Addams *(1860-1935), American social worker*

For what do we live, but to make sport for our neighbours, and laugh at them in our turn?
Jane Austen

We all live with the objective of being happy, our lives are all different and yet the same.
Anne Frank *(1929-45)*

LONELINESS/SOLITUDE

If I am such a legend, then why am I so lonely? If I'm such a legend, then why do I sit at home for hours staring at the damned telephone, hoping it's out of order, even calling the operator asking her if she's sure it's not out of order? Let me tell you legends are all very well if you've got somebody around who loves you, some man who's not afraid to be in love with Judy Garland.
Judy Garland *(1920-65), American actress*

I never said 'I want to be alone'. I only said 'I want to be let alone'.
Greta Garbo, *referring to the famous line in the film* Grand Hotel

To me, the sea is like a person – like a child that I've known a long time. It sounds crazy, I know, but when I swim in the sea I talk to it. I never feel alone when I'm out there.
Gertrude Ederle, *thirty years after becoming the first woman to swim the English Channel*

There are days when solitude is a heady wine that intoxicates you with freedom, others when it is a bitter tonic, and still others when it is a poison that makes you beat your head against the wall.
Colette, *'Freedom'*, Earthly Paradise, 1966

The person who tries to live alone will not succeed as a human being. His heart withers if it does not answer another heart. His mind shrinks away if he hears only the echoes of his own thoughts and finds no other inspiration.
Pearl Buck, 'To You on Your First Birthday', To My Daughters With Love, 1967

What a commentary on our civilisation, when being alone is considered suspect; when one has to apologise for it, make excuses, hide the fact that one practises it – like a secret vice.
Anne Morrow Lindbergh, 'Moon Shell', Gift From the Sea, 1955

Hell is oneself; hell is alone, the other figures in it merely projections. There is nothing to escape from and nothing to escape to. One is always alone.
George Eliot

Only in a house where one has learnt to be lonely does one have this solicitude for *things*. One's relation to them, the daily seeing or touching, begins to become love, and to lay one open to pain.
Elizabeth Bowen

On stage I make love to 25,000 people; then I go home alone.
Janis Joplin

What loneliness is more lonely than distrust?
George Eliot

L O V E

If love makes the world go round, why are we going to outer space?
Margaret Gilman

A narcissism shared by two.
Rita Mae Brown

The drug which makes sexuality palatable in popular mythology.
Germaine Greer

Don't threaten me with love baby.
Billie Holiday

Love: woman's eternal spring and man's eternal fall.
Helen Rowland

Love will never be ideal until man recovers from the
illusion that he can be just a little bit faithful or a little
bit married.
Helen Rowland

Some women and men seem to need each other.
Gloria Steinem

Falling out of love is very enlightening; for a short while
you see the world with new eyes.
Iris Murdoch

To fall in love you have to be in a state of mind for it to
take like a disease.
Nancy Mitford

If you can stay in love for more than two years, you're
on something.
Fran Lebowitz

The easiest kind of relationship for me is with ten
thousand people. The hardest is with one.
Joan Baez

Great passions don't exist – they are liars' fantasies.
What do exist are little loves that may last for a short or
longer while.
Anna Magnani (1918-73), *Italian actress*

I don't remember any love affairs. One must keep love
affairs quiet.
The Duchess of Windsor

The torch of love is lit in the kitchen.
French proverb

Love is much nicer to be in than an automobile
accident, a tight girdle, a higher tax bracket or a
holding pattern over Philadelphia.
Judith Viorist

A woman despises a man for loving her, unless she
returns his love.
Elizabeth Drew Stoddard (1823-1902), *American novelist and
poet*, Two Men

Love is moral even without legal marriage, but marriage is immoral without love.
Ellen Key, The Morality of Women

His generosity extended everywhere, to his friends, his family and the public. Every woman should have a Mike Todd in her life. God I loved him. My self esteem, my image, everything soared under his exuberant, loving care.
Elizabeth Taylor, Elizabeth Taylor Takes Off

I have had two great loves in my life. Mike Todd was the first.
Elizabeth Taylor

I don't want to live – I want to love first, and live incidentally . . .
Zelda Fitzgerald (then Sayre) (1900-48), American writer in a letter to her future husband, F. Scott Fitzgerald, 1919

Who so loves believes in the impossible.
Elizabeth Barrett Browning

It is said there is no happiness, and no love to be compared to that which is felt for the first time. Most persons erroneously think so; but love like other arts requires experience, and terror and ignorance, on its first approach, prevent our feeling it as strongly as at a later period.
Caroline Lamb (1785-1828), British novelist

Anyone must see at a glance that if men and women marry those whom they do not love, they must love those whom they do not marry.
Harriet Martineau (1802-76), British writer

It is the best of opiates.
Stevie Smith, British poet, Marriage I Think, 1937

Women who are content with light and easily broken ties do not *act* as I have done. They obtain what they desire and are still invited to dinner.
George Eliot, referring to her life with George Lewis

Raised me high, yet this I count the glory of my crown: that I have reigned with your loves.
Queen Elizabeth I in a speech to a deputation from the House of Commons, 1601

LOVE LETTERS

I will marry you so gladly with the old marriage service:
for better or worse in sickness and in health, and
forsaking all others – until death do us part, Ha! – Ha!
Dorothy Thompson *to her intended, Sinclair Lewis*

I am so anxious for you not to abdicate and I think the
fact that you do is going to put me in the wrong light to
the entire world because they will say that I could have
prevented it.
Wallis Simpson *to Edward VIII*

My life was better before I knew you.
Edith Wharton *to Morton Fullerton*

LOVERS

All really great lovers are articulate, and verbal
seduction is the surest road to actual seduction.
Marya Mannes

I wouldn't give up one minute of my time with Richard
Burton. We were like magnets, alternating pulling
towards each other and inexorably pushing away.
Elizabeth Taylor

Shall the dog lie where the deer once couched?
Nell Gwynn *(1650-87), English actress and mistress of Charles II,
refusing a lover after the King's death*

He's clearly the kind of chap who says, 'I'll be your
friend as well as your lover', never takes his eyes off you
as you walk towards him, always notices what you
wear and suggests doing all those things they do in the
movies, like walking hand in hand on the beach at
midnight, writing 'I love you' in the sand and having
champagne picnic breakfasts in the woods.
He says 'I want to know all about you', rings you in the
middle of the night, just to hear your voice, saturates
you with compliments, overwhelms you with roses, fills
you with confidence. He lifts your spirits as well as your
ego and then dumps you. Because it's his performance
as a charmer he's in love with – not with you.
Carla Lane, *TV scriptwriter, of her latest screen creation*

LOYALTY

The strongest bulwark of authority is uniformity; the least divergence from it is the greatest crime.
Emma Goldman *(1869-1940), American anarchist*

LUCK

Why is it no one ever sent me yet one perfect limousine, do you suppose? Ah, it's always my luck to get one perfect rose.
Dorothy Parker

Being in the right place at the right time in Europe, a person can achieve a lot.
Edwina Currie MP

LUST

Man in his lust has regulated long enough this whole question of sexual intercourse. Now let the mother of mankind, whose prerogative it is to set bounds to his indulgence, rouse up and give this whole matter a thorough, fearless examination.
Elizabeth Cady Stanton, *in a letter to Susan B. Anthony, 1853*

MALAPROPISMS

It's time to button down the hatches, or is it batten down the hedges?
Barbara Straus

He eats like a horse afire.
Angelina Bicos

They served the most abdominal cocktails.
Nellie Norton

MALICE

Malice is like a game of poker or tennis; you don't play it with anyone who is manifestly inferior to you.
Hilde Spiel

MARRIAGE

Marriage is a great institution, but I'm not ready for an institution.
Mae West

It was so cold I almost got married.
Shelley Winters

I married beneath me. All women do.
Nancy, Lady Astor (1879-1964)

Some of us are becoming the men we wanted to marry.
Gloria Steinem

When a girl marries, she exchanges the attentions of many men for the inattention of one.
Helen Rowland

Why does a woman work ten years to change a man's habits and then complain that he's not the man she married?
Barbra Streisand

Marriage always demands the greatest understanding of the art of insincerity possible between two human beings.
Vicki Baum

Before marriage, a man declares that he would lay down his life for you; after marriage, he won't even lay down his newspaper to talk to you.
Helen Rowland

Marrying a man is like buying something you've been admiring for a long time in a shop window. You may love it when you get it home, but it doesn't always go with everything else in the house.
Jean Kerr

I'd marry again if I found a man who had $15 million and would sign over half of it to me before the marriage, and guarantee he'd be dead within the year.
Bette Davis

A man in love is incomplete until he is married. Then he's finished.
Zsa Zsa Gabor

A book of which the first chapter is written in poetry
and the remaining chapters in prose.
Beverly Nichols

Almost all married people fight, although many are
ashamed to admit it. Actually a marriage in which no
quarrelling at all takes place may well be one that is
dead or dying from emotional undernourishment. If
you care, you probably fight.
Flora Davis

I feel sure that no girl could go to the altar, and would
probably *refuse*, if she knew *all* . . .
Queen Victoria

Happiness in marriage is entirely a matter of chance.
Jane Austen

Marriage is the deep, deep peace of the double bed after
the hurly-burly of the *chaise-longue*.
Mrs Patrick Campbell, British actress

God, for two people to be able to live together for the
rest of their lives is almost unnatural.
Jane Fonda

Marriage is a bargain, and somebody has to get the
worst of the bargain.
Helen Rowland

Any intelligent women who reads the marriage
contract, and then goes into it, deserves all the
consequences.
Isadora Duncan

Marriage was all a woman's idea, and for man's
acceptance of the pretty yoke it becomes us to be
grateful.
Phyllis McGinley, American poet

It is always incomprehensible to a man that a woman
should refuse an offer of marriage.
Jane Austen

Love-matches are made by people who are content, for
a month of honey, to condemn themselves to a life of
vinegar.
Marguerite, Countess of Blessington (1789-1849), Irish writer

People who haven't spoken to each other for years are on speaking terms again today – including the bride and groom.
Dorothy Parker, *on marrying Alan Campbell for the second time*

When you see what some girls marry, you realise how they must hate to work for a living.
Helen Rowland

It was just one of those things which, if you had been to bed before marriage, you would presumably have known.
Barbara Cartland

He's the kind of man a woman would have to marry to get rid of.
Mae West

I always say a girl must get married for love – and keep on getting married until she finds it.
Zsa Zsa Gabor *(currently on her eighth marriage)*

You, poor and obscure, and small and plain as you are – I entreat you to accept me as a husband.
Mr Rochester, *in* Jane Eyre *by Charlotte Brontë*

An engaged woman is always more agreeable than a disengaged. She is satisfied with herself. Her cares are over, and she feels that she may exert all her powers of pleasing without suspicion.
Jane Austen

Reader, I married him.
Charlotte Brontë

Among all the forms of absurd courage, the courage of girls is outstanding. Otherwise there would be fewer marriages.
Colette

I've married a few people I shouldn't have, but haven't we all?
Mamie Van Doren, *American actress*

It is true that I should have never married, but I didn't want to live without a man. Brought up to respect the conventions, love had to end in marriage. I'm afraid it did.
Bette Davis

I know a lot of people didn't expect our relationship to last – but we've just celebrated our two months anniversary.
Britt Ekland, *of her latest boyfriend*

Marriage: a souvenir of love.
Helen Rowland

Chains do not hold a marriage together. It is threads, hundreds of tiny threads which sew people together through the years. This is what makes a marriage last – more than passion or even sex!
Simone Signoret *(1921-85), French actress*

In no country, I believe, are the marriage laws so iniquitous as in England, and the conjugal relation, in consequence, so impaired.
Harriet Martineau *(1802-76), British writer,* Society in America

The early marriages of silly children . . . where . . . every woman is married before she well knows how serious a matter human life is.
Harriet Martineau

To marry a man out of pity is folly; and, if you think you are going to influence the kind of fellow who has 'never had a chance, poor devil', you are profoundly mistaken. One can only influence the strong characters in life, not the weak; and it is the height of vanity to suppose that you can make an honest man of anyone.
Margot Asquith *(1865-1945),* The Autobiography of Margot Asquith

A good marriage is at least 80 per cent good luck in finding the right person at the right time. The rest is trust.
Nanette Newman, *British actress*

After a few years of marriage a man can look right at a woman without seeing her and a woman can see right through a man without looking at him.
Helen Rowland

To Crystal, hair was the most important thing on earth. She would never get married because you couldn't wear curlers in bed.
Edna O'Brien, Winter's Tales

My marriage has given me confidence. I've always had support, it has improved the quality of my life. I'm very happy and very lucky.
Emma Thompson

I have been through marriage once and that's enough for the time being.
Jane Makim, *sister of the Duchess of York*

I have been around the world three times but I have not left Australia and no one has come to visit me.
Jane Makim, *in reply to journalists questioning her on the whereabouts of the Duchess of York (who disappeared for a few days after her separation from Prince Andrew)*

If there is any romance in marriage women must be given every chance to earn a decent living at other occupations. Otherwise no man can be sure that he is loved for himself alone, and that his wife did not come to the registry office because she had no luck at the labour exchange.
Rebecca West

The best thing for a woman to do is marry, have children and bring them up herself.
Elizabeth Lane, *British judge, in a speech at Malvern Girls' College, 1980*

MEMORIES

Better by far you should forget and smile, than you should remember and be sad.
Christina Rossetti

What a strange thing is memory, and hope; one looks backward, the other forward. The one is of today, the other is the tomorrow. Memory is history recorded in our brain, memory is a painter, it paints a picture of the past and of the day.
Grandma (Anna Mary Robertson) Moses *(1860-1961), American primitive painter*

We are well advised to keep on nodding terms with the people we used to be, whether we find them attractive company or not . . . we forget all too soon the things we thought we could never forget.
Joan Didion

Anyone who limits his vision to his memories of
yesterday is already dead.
Lily Langtry (1853-1929), British actress

MEN

Whenever I date a guy, I think, is this the man I want
my children to spend their weekends with?
Rita Rudner

One cannot be always laughing at a man without now
and then stumbling on something witty.
Jane Austen

Women want mediocre men, and men are working to
be as mediocre as possible.
Margaret Mead

Macho does not prove mucho.
Zsa Zsa Gabor

Some of my best leading men have been horses and
gods.
Elizabeth Taylor

Men who are insecure about their masculinity often
challenge me to fights.
Honor Blackman

Men are creatures with two legs and eight hands.
Jayne Mansfield

The male is a domestic animal which, if treated with
firmness and kindness, can be trained to do most things.
Jilly Cooper

He promised me earrings, but he only pierced my ears.
Arabian women's saying

I like men to behave like men – strong and childish.
Françoise Sagan

I only like two kinds of men: domestic and foreign.
Mae West

A man in the house is worth two in the street.
Mae West

He's the kind of bore who's here today and here tomorrow.
Binnie Barnes

I never hated a man enough to give him his diamonds back.
Zsa Zsa Gabor

I wish Frank Sinatra would just shut up and sing.
Lauren Bacall

I require only three things in a man: he must be handsome, ruthless and stupid.
Dorothy Parker

Never accept rides from strange men, and remember that all men are as strange as hell.
Robin Morgan

Where's a man who could ease a heart like a satin gown?
Dorothy Parker

He speaks to me as if I were a public meeting.
Queen Victoria *on Gladstone*

Harding was not a bad man, he was just a slob.
Alice Roosevelt Longworth

I refuse to consign the whole male sex to the nursery. I insist on believing that some men are my equals.
Brigitte Brophy

Men are beasts and even beasts don't behave as they do.
Brigitte Bardot

The more I see of men, the more I like dogs.
Madame de Staël

Giving a man space is like giving a dog a computer: the chances are he will not use it nicely.
Bette-Jane Raphael

The average man is more interested in a woman who is interested in him than he is in a woman with beautiful legs.
Marlene Dietrich

A man's heart may have a secret sanctuary where only one woman may enter, but it is full of little anterooms which are seldom vacant.
Helen Rowland

It's not the men in my life that counts, it's the life in my men.
Mae West

I love men like some people like good food or wine.
Germaine Greer

Give a man a free hand and he'll run it all over you.
Mae West

The penis is obviously going the way of the veriform appendix.
Jill Johnstone, American writer

None of you [men] ask for anything – except everything, but just for so long as you need it.
Doris Lessing

I'd never seen men hold each other. I thought the only thing they were allowed to do was shake hands or fight.
Rita Mae Brown

Probably the only place where a man can feel really secure is in a maximum security prison, except for the imminent threat of release.
Germaine Greer

The first time you buy a house you see how pretty the paint is and buy it. The second time you look to see if the basement has termites. It's the same with men.
Lupe Velez

I want a man who's kind and understanding. Is that too much to ask of a millionaire?
Zsa Zsa Gabor

To a smart girl men are no problem – they're the answer.
Zsa Zsa Gabor

The male sex, as a sex, does not universally appeal to me. I find the men today less manly; but a woman of my age is not in a position to know exactly how manly they are.
Katherine Hepburn

All men are rapists and that's all they are. They rape us with their laws and their codes.
Marilyn French

If men had more up top we'd need less up front.
Jaci Stephen

If man is only a little lower than the angels, the angels should reform.
Mary Wilson Little

There's nineteen men livin' in my neighbourhood, eighteen of them are fools and the one ain't no doggone good.
Bessie Smith

His mother should have thrown him away and kept the stork.
Mae West

Mad, bad and dangerous to know.
Lady Caroline Lamb (1785-1828), *British novelist, on Byron*

Mountains appear more lofty the nearer they are approached, but great men resemble them not in this particular.
The Countess of Blessington (1789-1849), *Irish writer*

It's a man's world, and you men can have it.
Katherine Ann Porter (1890-1980), *American writer*

When I saw him sitting behind his desk in his opulent office he looked just like Blake Carrington.
Fiona Wright, *on Sir Ralph Halpern*

We seek him here, we seek him there
Those Frenchies seek him everywhere.
Is he in heaven? – Is he in hell?
That damned elusive Pimpernel.
Baroness Orczy (1865-1947), *British novelist*, The Scarlet Pimpernel

If Kitchener was not a great man, he was, at least, a good poster.
Margot Asquith, *the second wife of Herbert Asquith*

The last gentleman in Europe.
Ada Beddington Leverson (1862-1933), *British writer, on Oscar Wilde*

If men had to have babies, they would only ever have one each.
Diana, Princess of Wales

I am partial to ladies if they are nice. I suppose it is my nature. I am not quite a gentleman but you would hardly notice it.
Daisy Ashford (1881-1972), British writer of The Young Visitors, *aged 9*

One hell of an outlay for a very small return with most of them.
Glenda Jackson

A hard man's good to find – but you'll mostly find him asleep.
Mae West

There is a vast difference between the savage and the civilised man, but it is never apparent to their wives until after breakfast.
Helen Rowland

How can a woman scruple entire subjection, how can she forbear to admire the worth and excellency of a superior sex, if she at all considers it? Have not all the great actions that have been performed in the world been done by men? Have not they founded empires and overturned them? Do not they make laws and continually repeal and amend them? Their vast minds lay kingdoms waste, no bounds or measures can be prescrib'd to their desires . . . they make worlds and ruin them, form systems of universal nature and dispute eternally about them; their pen gives worth to the most trifling controversy . . .
Mary Astell (1666-1737), English feminist writer

I like men macho rather than caring or sensitive.
Jilly Cooper

The male is a biological accident: the Y (male) gene is an incomplete X (female) gene, that is, has an incomplete set of chromosomes. In other words, the male is an incomplete female, a walking abortion, aborted at the gene stage.
Valerie Solanas, SCUM manifesto, 1967

Words such as 'beast', 'brute', 'monster' and 'sex fiend' are commonly used to describe the rapist. Yet we rarely see the simple word 'man' which the rapist invariably is.
Cambridge Rape Crisis Centre, Out of Focus, 1987

We love them and we hate them! But it would be rather
boring without them!
Evelln Klose

They say it is a man's world, but ask any man.
Anon

Bloody Men are like bloody buses –
you wait for about a year
and as soon as one approaches your stop
two or three others appear.

You look at them flashing their indicators,
offering you a ride.
You're trying to read the destinations,
you haven't much time to decide.

If you make a mistake, there is no turning back.
Jump off and you'll stand there and gaze
while the cars and the taxis and lorries go by
and the minutes, the hours and days.
Wendy Cope, Bloody Men

M E N O P A U S E

What happens during the climacteric is that the people
she has served all her life stop making demands on her.
She becomes a moon without an earth. What she wants
is to be wanted and nobody wants her.
Germaine Greer, The Change, 1991

M I N D

Anything we can conceive, we can achieve – the most
underdeveloped territory in the world is under our
scalps and I would that we have calluses on our minds
but not bunions on our countryside.
Dorothy M. Carl

The brain is as strong as its weakest think.
Eleanor Doan

M I S T R E S S E S

One of Edward's mistresses was Jane Shore, who has
had a play written about her, but it was a tragedy and
therefore not worth reading.
Jane Austen

MODESTY

I wasn't really naked. I simply didn't have any clothes on.
Josephine Baker

I have often wished I had time to cultivate modesty . . . but I am too busy thinking about myself.
Dame Edith Sitwell (1887-1964), British writer

MOMENTS

Bad moments, like good ones, tend to be grouped together.
Edna O'Brien

Every now and then when you're on stage, you hear the best sound a player can hear. It's a sound you can't get in movies or television. It is the sound of a wonderful, deep silence that means you've hit them where they live.
Shelley Winters

I'm not easily embarrassed and I don't regard stepping down from the Department of Health as embarrassing, it was a row waiting to happen. One thing did happen recently, though. I was trying on a skirt in the sales when the fitting-room curtain was pulled back. Three faces appeared and started arguing, saying: 'It is her. No it isn't. Yes it is.'
Edwina Currie MP

MONEY

I believe in the dollar. Everything I earn, I spend!
Joan Crawford

Too much of a good thing can be wonderful.
Mae West

Where large sums of money are concerned, it is advisable to trust nobody.
Agatha Christie

Having money is rather like being blonde. It's more fun but not vital.
Mary Quant

Money is always there but the pockets change; it is not the same pockets after a change, and that is all there is to say about money.
Gertrude Stein

There are poor men in this country who cannot be bought; the day I found that out, I sent my gold abroad.
Comtesse de Voigrand

Keep cool and collect.
Mae West

I've been rich and I've been poor – rich is better.
Sophie Tucker

The only thing I like about rich people is their money.
Lady Astor

Wealth without virtue
is a harmful companion
but a mixture of both,
the happiest friendship.
Sappho, Greek poet who lived during the sixth century BC

There will never be enough money when you follow what is right.
Phyllis Carter

I do want to get rich but I never want to do what there is to do to get rich.
Gertrude Stein

Some people are more turned on by money than they are by love. In one respect they're alike. They're both wonderful as long as they last.
Abigail Van Buren

There are dozens of ways of failing to make money. It is one thing to fail to make money because your single talent happens to be a flair amounting to genius for translating the plays of Aristophanes. It is quite another thing to fail to make money because you are black, or a child, or a woman.
Margaret Halsey

I never had any money till I took off my pants.
Sally Rand (1884-1966), American dancer and entertainer

Money speaks sense in a language that all nations understand.
Aphra Behn (1640-89), *the first Englishwoman to make a career in letters*

Algebra and money are essentially levellers; the first intellectually, the second effectively.
Simone Weil, *French philosopher*

I have known many persons who turned their gold into smoke, but you are the first to turn smoke into gold.
Queen Elizabeth I *to Sir Walter Raleigh on his introducing tobacco to Britain*

People think that all polo players must be very wealthy and they don't realise that a lot of people make huge sacrifices for the sport. I know people who've ended up living in flats just to keep their polo ponies going.
Janie McLean, *wife of oil trader Neil*

We don't pay taxes. Only little people pay taxes.
Leona Helmsley, *New York hotel owner, who was found guilty of tax evasion in 1989*

I would feel desperate if I had been without a good regular income for 20 years.
Margaret Thatcher

Press reports about how much people like us earn are usually wildly exaggerated. But people do believe that being on the telly is essentially a frivolous job – I don't think anyone gets resentful about brain surgeons being paid a lot. I can see the point. On the other hand, presenting's a lot harder than you might think, it's enormously stressful and a very definite skill. It's also worth remembering that it's a short life. You're only a television presenter for as long as your face fits. There's no guarantee your job's going to last. So, basically, you earn while you can.
Judy Finnigan, *presenter of* This Morning, *on being asked if she thought TV presenters were overpaid*

Anyone who makes a lot of money quickly must be pretty crooked – honest pushing away at the grindstone never made anyone a bomb.
Mandy Rice-Davies, *who was at the centre of the Profumo scandal of 1963*

In the midst of life we are in debt.
Ethel Watts Mumford (1878-1940), American writer

M O O D S

Before I met him, I wasn't used to the fact that buying
the wrong length shoelaces would be reason to
contemplate suicide.
*Sarah Wood, estranged wife of actor James Wood, talking about
his moodiness*

M O R A L I T Y

I am pure as the driven slush.
Tallulah Bankhead

Love is moral even without legal marriage, but marriage
is immoral without love.
Ellen Key

There is nothing immoral in my books, only murder.
Agatha Christie

M O T H E R S   A N D
M O T H E R H O O D

If I had been the Virgin Mary, I would have said no.
Stevie Smith

Women who miscalculate are called mothers.
Abigail Van Buren

It takes a women twenty years to make a man of her
son and another woman twenty minutes to make a fool
of him.
Helen Rowland (1876-1950)

I had to censor everything my son watched . . . even on
the Mary Tyler Moore show I heard the word damn!
Mary Lou Bax

Instant availability without continuous presence is
probably the best role a mother can play.
Lotte Bailyn

I'm not against mothers. I am against the ideology which expects every woman to have children, and I'm against the circumstances under which mothers have to have their children.
Simone de Beauvoir

It is neither necessary nor just to make it imperative on women that they should either be mothers or nothing, or that if they have been mothers they should be nothing else during the whole remainder of their lives.
Harriet Taylor

Devoted grandmother though I am now, I strongly resent the assumption that our capacity for childbearing and our natural inclination towards childcare and child-rearing are the only reasons for our being here on the earth.
Mary Stott

In search of my mother's garden I found my own.
Alice Walker, American writer

I always thought I'd become more independent as they got older. But it doesn't work like that. I think that all new mothers imagine their baby can't survive without them, but in fact someone else can look after the baby unless you're breast-feeding. It's when they get older that the parents assume a more special role. Other people can't really help with growing-up problems, homework or giving your children the continuity and stability they need in their lives.
Carol Barnes, ITN newsreader

Giving birth to Lola was the most wonderful moment of my life. She's everything I ever hoped for.
Annie Lennox

It has changed my life and my perspective on things in all the corny ways that children are supposed to.
Annie Lennox

Having a child doesn't so much change your priorities as set them straight. But once I start to talk about it, I'm liable to come out with every cliché in the book. The experience is so intense and personal that you end up thinking you're the only person it's ever happened to.
Annie Lennox

Mother is the dead heart of the family, spending Father's earnings on consumer goods to enhance the environment in which he eats, sleeps and watches the television.
Germaine Greer, *Australian-born British writer and feminist,* The Female Eunuch

Motherhood is the most emotional experience of one's life. One joins a kind of women's mafia.
Janet Suzman

With animals you don't see the male caring for the offspring. It's against nature. It is a woman's prerogative and duty, and a privilege.
Princess Grace of Monaco *(1928-82)*

If you bungle raising your children, I don't think whatever else you do will matter very much.
Jacqueline Kennedy Onassis

I became this very defensive woman, giving up everything just to stay at home and be with Billie.
Dawn French, *actress, on her child*

Sometimes we blame Mom too much for all that is wrong with her sons and daughters. After all, we might well ask, who started the grim mess? Who, long ago made Mom and her sex 'inferior' and stripped her of her economic and political and sexual rights?
Lillian Smith *(1897-1966), American writer and social critic*

No matter how old a mother is, she watches her middle-aged children for signs of improvement.
Florida Scott-Maxwell, American-born British writer, psychologist, playwright, suffragette and actress

These love children always suffer because their mothers have crushed them under their stays trying to hide them, more's the pity. Yet after all, a lovely unrepentant creature, but with child is not such an outrageous sight.
Colette, My Mother's House, *1922*

I believe as a wage earning woman, that if I make the great sacrifice of strength and health and even risk my life, to have a child, I should certainly not do so if, on some future occasion, the man can say that the child belongs to him by law and he will take it from me and I shall see it only three times a year!
Isadora Duncan (1878-1927), American dancer, My Life, *1927*

Mothers who can share their children's interests, mothers who have some knowledge of the wider world outside the family circle, are far better equipped than purely domestic housewives, to help their sons and daughters as they pass from school to the shops and offices and factories and universities in which they complete their education.
Winifred Hotby (1898-1935), British writer, Women and Changing Civilisation, *1934*

It is misleading and unfair to imply that an intelligent woman must 'rise above' her maternal instincts and return to work when many intelligent, sensitive women have found that the reverse is better for them.
Sally E. Shaywitz, American paediatrician and writer, Catch 22 for Mothers, *1973*

My first child was born in 1967 when I was twenty-two and had accomplished a university degree. I thought it was my vocation to be a mother . . . but the time that followed was an unhappy haze of nappy-washing and pill-taking, as I found I could not make my dream of domestic contentment come true. I felt depressed and oppressed. I felt constantly tired. I felt isolated. I felt resentful of my husband's freedom. I felt my life was at an end.
Ann Oakley, British sociologist, From Here to Maternity, *1981*

A mother, if physically capable, whether regal or otherwise, ought to supply nature's food to her own offspring.

A letter to the Lancet *in 1840 referring to Queen Victoria's refusal to breastfeed her children*

M U S I C

I always wish that the last movement [of the Regenlieder Sonata] might accompany me in my journey from here to the next world.

Clara Schumann *(1819-96), German pianist, to Brahms*

I wish the government would put a tax on pianos for the incompetent.

Dame Edith Sitwell

For instrumental music there is a certain Haydn, who has some peculiar ideas, but he is only just beginning.

Maria Theresa *(1717-80), Empress and Ruler of the Habsburg Dominions, in a letter to Archduchess Marie Beatrix, 1772*

You ask my opinion about taking the young Salzburg musician Mozart into your service. I do not know where you can place him, since I feel that you do not require a composer or any other useless people... it gives one's service a bad name, when such types go about the world like beggars; besides, he has a large family.

Maria Theresa *in a letter to her son*

Nobody really sings in an opera – they just make loud noises.

Amelita Galli-Curci *(1889-1963), Italian singer*

My playing is getting all behindhand, as is always the case when Robert is composing. I cannot find one little hour in the day for myself.

Clare Schumann, *on her husband Robert*

I know the song and I can make all those noises at home.

Queen Elizabeth I

Music is not written in red, white and blue. It is written in the heart's blood of the composer.

Nellie Melba, *Australian soprano*

Music has always been my lover. And such a part of me that whoever wanted me wanted me with the music.
Montserrat Caballe

When music fails to agree to the ear, to soothe the ear and the heart and the senses, then it has missed its point.
Maria Callas (1923-77), *Greek opera singer*

I haven't done that in 20 years. Let's open a bottle of champagne.
Evelyn Laye, on hitting an F sharp

NATIONALITY

As a woman I have no country, as a woman I want no country. As a woman my country is the whole world.
Virginia Woolf

America is my country, and Paris is my home town, and it is as it has come to be. After all, anybody is as their land and air is. Anybody is as the sky is low or high, the air heavy or clear, and anybody is as there is wind or no wind there. It is that which makes them and the arts they make and the work they do and the way they eat and the way they drink and the way they learn and everything. And so I am an American and I have lived half my life in Paris, not the half of me that made me, but the half in which I made what I made.
Gertrude Stein

The longer I live the more I turn to New Zealand. I thank God I was born in New Zealand. A young country is a real heritage, though it takes one time to recognise it. But New Zealand is in my very bones.
Katherine Mansfield

If I were an Australian, I would be thinking very hard about the problem and what they are going to do.
The Duchess of Kent, joining in the debate on whether Australia should become a republic

When I die I'd like to be buried in Paris, and I'd also like to leave my heart in England. But in Germany – nothing.
Marlene Dietrich

Women are all one nation.
Turkish proverb

OPINION

Opinions differ most when there is least scientific
warrant for having any.
Daisy Bates

Men get opinions as boys learn to spell. By reiteration
chiefly.
Elizabeth Barrett Browning

It is just when opinions universally prevail and we have
added lip service to their authority that we become
sometimes most keenly conscious that we do not believe
a word that we are saying.
Virginia Woolf, The Common Reader

The English think of an opinion as something which a
decent person, if he has the misfortune to have one,
does all he can to hide.
Margaret Halsey, With Malice Toward Some

There is nothing a woman so dislikes as to have her old
opinions quoted to her, especially when they confute
new ones.
Katherine Tynan Hinkson (1861-1931), Irish poet and novelist

Notwithstanding all my violence in politics, and talking
so much on that subject, I perfectly agree with you that
no woman has any business to meddle with that or any
other serious business, farther than giving her opinion
(if she is asked).
Lady Besseborough in a letter to Lord Granville

OPPORTUNITY

Opportunities are usually disguised as hard work, so
most people don't recognise them.
Ann Landers

Too often, the opportunity knocks, but by the time you
push back the chain, push back the bolt, unhook the
two locks and shut off the burglar alarm, it's too late.
Rita Coolidge, American singer

One doesn't recognise in one's life the really important moment – not until it's too late.
Agatha Christie

If your only opportunity is to be equal, then it is not opportunity.
Margaret Thatcher

One can present people with opportunities. One cannot make them equal to them.
Rosamond Lehmann, British novelist, The Ballad and the Source

I had to think quite hard about that . . . but I felt that if Chris really wanted to do it there were really enough opportunities and exciting possibilities for me too.
Lavender Patten, on the prospect of her husband Chris taking up the post of Governor of Hong Kong

The only way out is through.
Helen Keller

O P T I M I S M

Now we can look the East End in the face.
Queen Elizabeth the Queen Mother, surveying the damage caused to Buckingham Palace by a bomb during the blitz

P A I N

Pain is the root of knowledge.
Simone Weil

Beauty cannot disguise nor music melt
a pain undiagnosable but felt.
Anne Morrow Lindbergh, The Stone

It is the unknown of the black pit of suffering that breeds fear, and makes people run away from their own suffering and deny the suffering of others.
Nicolette Devas

Corporal punishment is as humiliating for him who gives it as for him who receives it; it is ineffective besides. Neither shame nor physical pain have any other effect than a hardening one . . .
Ellen Key, The Century of the Child

Flowers grow out of dark moments.
Corita Kent

PANIC

It's more than panic, it's a kind of desperation which
you have to keep at bay, otherwise it's ugly. And the
only way you're going to learn how to be cool while
you're doing it, is to do it. I was sick about doing a
one-woman show, and I ended up touring with it.
Coolness takes over.
Ruby Wax, on whether she feels panic before going on stage

PASSIONS

I've always admitted that I'm ruled by my passions.
Elizabeth Taylor

PAST

Everyone is the child of his past.
Edna G. Rostow

We are tomorrow's past.
Mary Webb

The past was nothing to her; offered no lesson which
she was willing to heed. The future was a mystery
which she never attempted to penetrate. The present
alone was significant . . .
Kate Chopin (1851-1904), The Awakening

Each has his past shut in him like the leaves of a book
known to him by heart and his friends can only read the
title.
Virginia Woolf, Jacob's Room

PEACE

I am no lover of pompous title, but only desire that my
name be recorded in a line or two, which shall briefly
express my name, my virginity, the years of my reign,
the reformation of religion under it, and my
preservation of peace.
Queen Elizabeth I

We are the true peace movement.
Margaret Thatcher

PENIS

A man is two people, himself and his cock. A man
always takes his friend to the party. Of the two, the
friend is the nicer, being more able to show his feelings.
Beryl Bainbridge, *English novelist*

I wonder why men get serious at all. They have this
delicate long thing hanging outside their bodies which
goes up and down by its own will. If I were a man I
would always be laughing at myself.
Yoko Ono

Keithley Miller (an American lady) asked a Scotsman
whether it was true that they wore nothing under their
kilts. Lifting up his kilt, the (somewhat inebriated) Scot
revealed all and asked 'What do you think of that?' She
replied: 'Well, it looks like a penis . . . only smaller'.
Anon

PHILOSOPHY

A philosophy is characterised more by the formulation
of its problems than by the solution to them.
Anon

I have a simple philosophy. Fill what's empty. Empty
what's full. Scratch where it itches.
Alice Roosevelt Longworth *(1884-1980)*

PHOTOGRAPHY

A photograph is a secret about a secret. The more it
tells you the less you know.
Diane Arbus *(1923-71), American photographer*

While there is perhaps a province in which the
photograph can tell us nothing more than what we see
with our own eyes, there is another in which it proves
to us how little our eyes permit us to see.
Dorothea Lange *(1895-1963), American photographer*

You won't need me now you've got Fergie.
Princess Diana *to a group of photographers*

PLASTIC SURGERY

You have to feel sympathy for the Florida woman who is suing her doctor after she ended up with four breasts following cosmetic surgery. Dr Dedo, she later discovered, was an ear, nose and throat specialist.
Jaci Stephen

People say you shouldn't have plastic surgery because if God wanted you another way he would have made you that way, but I say that's a lot of crock. If God didn't want plastic surgeons, he wouldn't have given them hands to work with.
Dolly Parton

PLEASURE

One half of the world cannot understand the pleasures of the other.
Jane Austen

Few pleasures there are indeed without an aftertouch of pain, but that is the preservation which keeps them sweet.
Helen Keller

Variety is the soul of pleasure.
Aphra Behn

POETRY

. . . Poetry, 'The Cinderella of the Arts'.
Harriet Monrow *(1860-1936), American poet and editor,* Famous American Women

The poet gives us his essence, but prose takes the mould of the body and mind entire.
Virginia Woolf, The Captain's Death Bed

My poems are hymns of praise to the glory of life.
Dame Edith Sitwell

Who shall measure the heat and violence of the poet's heart when caught and tangled in a woman's body?
Virginia Woolf

Correct English is the slang of the prigs who write history and essays. And the strongest slang of all is the slang of poets.
George Eliot

When I feel physically as if the top of my head were taken off, I know that it is poetry.
Emily Dickinson

POLITICS

Tories are not always wrong, but they are always wrong at the right moment.
Lady Violet Bonham-Carter (1887-1969), president of the Liberal Party, 1945-47

Ninety-eight per cent of adults in this country are decent, hard-working, honest Americans. It's the other lousy two per cent that get all the publicity. But then – we elected them.
Lily Tomlin

One of the things that politics has taught me is that men are not a reasoned or reasonable sex.
Margaret Thatcher

Never lose your temper with the press or the public is a major rule of political life.
Christabel Pankhurst (1880-1958), British suffragette

The reason there are so few female politicians is that it is too much trouble to put make-up on two faces.
Maureen Murphy, former Labour MP

If you weren't such a great man you'd be a terrible bore.
Mrs William Gladstone, to her husband

The First Lady is an unpaid public servant elected by one person – her husband.
Lady Bird Johnston

The public is entitled to know whether or not I am married to Jack the Ripper.
Geraldine Ferraro, American politician

Sure Reagan promised to take senility tests. But what if he forgets?
Lorna Kerr-Walker

Its [The Democratic Party's] leaders are always troubadours of trouble: crooners of catastrophe . . . A Democratic president is doomed to proceed to his goals like a squid, squirting darkness all around him.
Clare Booth Luce, American diplomat

They say women talk too much. If you have worked in Congress you know that the filibuster was invented by men.
Clare Booth Luce

Perhaps this country needs an Iron Lady.
Margaret Thatcher

I don't understand that. I have the right to vote. I pay my taxes. The voters will make up their own minds. What people care about is where Labour stands.
Glenda Jackson MP, replying to charges that she used her celebrity status as an election weapon, March 1992

I am firm. You are obstinate. He is a pigheaded fool.
Katherine Whitehorn

Communism is the opiate of the intellectuals.
Clare Boothe Luce

In politics, if you want anything said, ask a man; if you want anything done, ask a woman.
Margaret Thatcher

No one has ever so comforted the distressed – or so distressed the comfortable.
Clare Boothe Luce on Eleanor Roosevelt

Is there life after the White House?
Betty Ford

I have sacrificed everything in my life that I consider precious in order to advance the political career of my husband.
Pat Nixon

Richard Nixon impeached himself. He gave us Gerald Ford as his revenge.
Bella Abzug, American politician

My long-term goal is to see Britain free from socialism.
Margaret Thatcher, May 1987

We had to fight the enemy without in the Falklands. We always have to be aware of the enemy within, which is more difficult to fight and more dangerous to liberty.
Margaret Thatcher, on the Miners' Strike of 1984-85

Beer and sandwiches at No. 10? No, never.
Margaret Thatcher, at the time of the Miners' Strike

He says he won't be devastated if he loses, but I think that would be difficult. I think about it quite a lot, actually.
Norma Major, on John Major in the run-up to the 1992 election

Britain is no longer in the politics of the pendulum, but of the ratchet.
Margaret Thatcher

And I don't feel the attraction of the Kennedys at all ... I don't think they are Christians; they may be Catholics but they are not Christians.
Mary McCarthy, American novelist

Margaret Thatcher is David Owen in drag.
The Rhodesia Herald, *August 1979*

I love argument, I love debate. I don't expect anyone just to sit there and agree with me, that's not their job.
Margaret Thatcher

U-turn if you want to. The lady's not for turning.
Margaret Thatcher

And what prize do we have to fight for? No less than the chance to banish from our land the dark divisive clouds of Marxist socialism.
Margaret Thatcher

State socialism is totally alien to the British character.
Margaret Thatcher

I can't wait to be on the other side of it, actually. It's been in sight ever since John became Prime Minister – we've all been waiting for it a long time.
Norma Major, on being asked if she was looking forward to the General Election

Some criticism of him is unfair and it makes me bloody angry, but it doesn't last long. I know that if you put yourself forward you're in line for criticism. I love *Spitting Image* and *Week Ending* – thank God for the great British sense of humour.
Jane Ashdown, on how she copes with the personal and political criticism of her husband

What's the first thing you'll say to him on the morning after the general election, 1992?

Well, this is the first day of the rest of our lives.
Norma Major

We made it!
Glenys Kinnock

Let's go on a holiday, you need a rest.
Jane Ashdown

I've always been a teacher and I love it. I teach two days a week and perhaps I'd have done more if Neil hadn't been in politics. But I have no regrets.
Glenys Kinnock

I am certain that we will win the election with a good majority. Not that I am ever overconfident.
Margaret Thatcher

During the last few weeks I have felt that the Suez canal was flowing through my drawing room.
Clarissa Eden (1920-85), wife of Anthony Eden

Margaret Thatcher's great strength seems to be the better people know her, the better they like her. But, of course, she has one great disadvantage – she is a daughter of the people and looks trim, as the daughters of the people desire to be. Shirley Williams has such an advantage over her because she's a member of the upper-middle class and can achieve that kitchen-sink-revolutionary look that one cannot get unless one has been to a really good school.
Rebecca West

I cannot and will not cut my conscience to fit this year's fashions even though I long ago came to the conclusion that I was not a political person and could have no comfortable place in any political group.
Lillian Hellman, in a letter to the House of Representatives Committee on Un-American Activities, May 1952

Nobody knows me. Why should they? I just tell people I'm the one who looks like Edwina Currie.
Gillian Shepherd MP, Employment Secretary, April 1992

We're an ideal political family, as accessible as Disneyland.
Maureen Reagan, daughter of President Reagan

Yes, entirely true. I think these situations always end in tears. Margaret Thatcher, David Owen . . . I knew that I would give my husband to the party.
Jane Ashdown, on being asked whether it was true she had not wanted her husband to lead the Liberal Democrats.

I'll stay until I'm tired of it. So long as Britain needs me I shall never be tired of it.
Margaret Thatcher

It was then that the iron entered my soul.
Margaret Thatcher, on her time in Edward Heath's Cabinet

Having consulted widely among colleagues, I have concluded that the unity of the party and the prospects of victory in a general election would be better served if I stood down to enable Cabinet colleagues to enter the ballot for the leadership.
Margaret Thatcher, November 1990

I am the lady who says there aren't more women MPs because we've got more sense.
Jean Denton

She could well have resented younger women like myself coming and joining her in the Cabinet after she had put in such a long period of slogging work during her period in opposition, but she didn't, she was not at all resentful about it.
Shirley Williams on Barbara Castle

There exists no politician in India daring enough to attempt to explain to the masses that cows can be eaten.
Indira Gandhi (1917-84)

If we are to reinvigorate the party, and if we are to attract new members, we must guarantee them a clear voice in the decision-making process.
Margaret Beckett MP, deputy leader of the Labour Party

Power-hungry federalists will turn Europe into a monstrous puppet ruled by Germany . . .
The day of the artificially constructed megastate has gone. So the Euro-federalists are now desperately scurrying to build one.
Margaret Thatcher

It's still disconcerting to be aware of cameras watching me all the time.
Norma Major

We're fair game but the children aren't.
Norma Major on Press attention

We dealt with the unions. We privatised things. We went to the Falklands and we were the first to go to the Gulf. All accomplished with action and enterprise.
Margaret Thatcher

My castaway this week is a politician. His background and childhood are well known. Indeed his humble origins are part of the reason why, just over a year ago, he was elected leader of his party. His characteristics are familiar too. He is self-effacing but he must be ambitious.
Sue Lawley, on John Major, Desert Island Discs, January 1992

Put a sock in it Peter, the debate's over now. After about seven minutes I carefully tipped my orange juice over his head. It did the trick.
Edwina Currie MP, of her reaction to Peter Snape, Labour Transport Spokesman, in Central TV's Birmingham Studios.

I like to win a fight. I like to be bloodied and victorious. I think the fire has gone out of politics in this country. I get out of bed in the morning to fight socialism and the real battle is taking place in Europe.
Edwina Currie MP

The last time I started a new job I got a desk and telephone, as well as a stapler, pencil sharpener and rubber. No such wealth of provision greets a new MP.
Lynne Jones MP, on her first day at Westminster, 1992.

I was quite unprepared for the shock at the start of my first Parliamentary Labour Party meeting. Neil Kinnock entered and the room erupted with the banging of fists on tables. Did Labour Party members really behave in this way? Not being used to the ways of public schools, I clapped politely.
Lynne Jones MP

POTENTIAL

Society in its full sense . . . is never an entity separable from the individuals who compose it. No individual can arrive even at the threshold of his potential without a culture in which he participates. Conversely, no civilisation has in it any element which in the last analysis is not the contribution of an individual.
Ruth Benedict

The becoming of man is the history of the exhaustion of his possibilities.
Susan Sontag, Styles of the Radical Will, 1969

You know what you can do best, and you know what is the best that you do.
Margaret Thatcher, to Prof. Sir Alan Walters *when she appointed him as her economic adviser*

POVERTY

Every stable government in history has depended on the resignation of the poor to being poor.
Felicité de Lamennais (1782-1854)

America is an enormous frosted cupcake in the middle of millions of starving people.
Gloria Steinem

I have the impression that when we talk so confidently of liberty we are unaware of the awful servitude . . . of poverty when means are so small that there is literally no choice.
Barbara Ward

Single women have a dreadful propensity to being poor.
Jane Austen

One must be poor to know the luxury of giving.
George Eliot

I was very sad for many days when I discovered that in the world there were poor people and rich people; and the strange thing is that the existence of the poor did not cause me as much pain as the knowledge that at the same time there were people who were rich.
Eva Perón (1919-52), *Argentine politician,* My Life's Cause

POWER

I am a woman in the prime of life, with certain powers and those powers severely limited by authorities whose faces I rarely see.
Adrienne Rich, *American poet*

Powerlessness corrupts. Absolute powerlessness corrupts absolutely.
Professor Rosabeth Moss Kanter, *Harvard Business School, May 1991*

We have never yet had a Labour government that knew what taking power really means; they always act like second-class citizens.
Doris Russell (1894-1986), *British author and campaigner*

PREGNANCY

If I had a cock for a day I would get myself pregnant.
Germaine Greer

If pregnancy were a book they would cut the last two chapters.
Nora Ephron

I've become more mature and responsible. I feel womanly. It's an intense pleasure.
Princess Stephanie of Monaco, *on her first pregnancy*

PREJUDICE

Law is a reflection and source of prejudice. It both enforces and suggests forms of bias.
Diane Schulder

Nobody outside a baby-carriage or a judge's chamber believes in an unprejudiced point of view.
Lillian Hellman

The trouble with our people is as soon as they got out of slavery they didn't want to give the white man nothing else. But the fact is, you got to give 'em something. Either your money, your land, your woman or your ass.
Alice Walker, American author and critic

Race prejudice is not only a shadow over the coloured – it is a shadow over all of us, and the shadow is darkest over those who feel it least and allow its evil effects to go on.
Pearl Buck (1892-1973), American novelist

The truth is that Mozart, Pascal, Bolean algebra, Shakespeare, parliamentary government, baroque churches, Newton, the emancipation of women, Kant, Marx, and Ballanchine ballets don't redeem what this particular civilisation has wrought upon the world. The white race is the cancer of human history.
Susan Sontag

PRIDE

I'll keep my personal dignity and pride to the very end – it's all I have left and it's a possession that only myself can part with.
Daisy Bates

PROGRESS

The biggest sin is sitting on your ass.
Florynce Kennedy

I was taught the way of progress is neither swift nor easy.
Marie Curie

'How wonderful it must have been for the ancient Britons,' my mother said once, 'when the Romans arrived they could have a hot bath.'
Katherine Whitehorn

PSYCHIATRY

One should only see a psychiatrist out of boredom.
Muriel Spark

PUNISHMENT

Punishment is not for revenge, but to lessen crime and reform the criminal.
Elizabeth Fry (1780-1845), *British social reformer*

QUESTIONS

The shortest answer is doing.
English proverb

There is really nothing more to say – except why. But since why is difficult to handle, one must take refuge in how.
Toni Morrison, *American writer*

How do you like what you have? This is a question that anybody can ask anybody. Ask it.
Gertrude Stein

I can honestly say that I was never affected by the question of the success of an undertaking if I felt it was the right thing to do. I was for it regardless of the possible outcome.
Golda Meir

We intend to remain alive. Our neighbours want to see us dead. This is not a question that leaves much room for compromise.
Golda Meir

REALITY

Reality is a crutch for people who can't cope with drugs.
Lily Tomlin

REASON

I'll not listen to reason . . . reason always means what someone else has got to say.
Mrs E. C. Gaskell (1810-65), English novelist and biographer

REGRET

Make it a rule of life never to regret and never to look back. Regret is an appalling waste of energy: you can't build on it; it is good only for wallowing in.
Katherine Mansfield

The follies which a man regrets most in his life are those which he didn't commit when he had the opportunity.
Helen Rowland (1876-1950), Reflections of a Bachelor Girl

RELATIONSHIPS

I tend to be suspicious of people whose love of animals is exaggerated; they are often frustrated in their relationships with humans.
Ylla (Camilla Koffler)

There are a lot of men who will ask me out just to be seen with a celebrity.
Elizabeth Taylor

RELIGION

A converted cannibal is one who, on Friday, eats only fishermen.
Emily Lotney

I don't believe in God but I do believe in his saints.
Edith Wharton

God is a living doll.
Jane Russell

Most of my friends are not Christians, but I have some who are Anglicans or Roman Catholics.
Dame Rose Macauley

I went to a convent in New York and was fired finally for my insistence that the Immaculate Conception was a spontaneous combustion.
Dorothy Parker

When we talk to God, we're praying. When God talks to us we're schizophrenic.
Lily Tomlin

God is love, but get it in writing.
Gypsy Rose Lee, American entertainer and writer

Religion is love; in no case is it logic.
Beatrice Webb (1858-1943), British writer and economist, My Apprenticeship

There is no sinner like a young saint.
Aphra Behn

Parsons always seem to be specially horrified about things like sunbathing and naked bodies. They don't mind poverty and misery and cruelty to animals nearly as much.
Susan Ertz (1894-1985), British novelist

Place before your eyes two precepts, and only two. One is preach the Gospel; and the other is – put down enthusiasm . . . The Church of England in a nutshell.
Mrs Humphrey Ward (1851-1920), British novelist

Before confession, be perfectly sure that you do not wish to be forgiven.
Katherine Mansfield, New Zealand-born writer

When I first thought of becoming a rabbi, it was the intellectual and academic side that appealed. But when I was sent off to various congregations as a student, I really enjoyed it – so in the end I became a congregational rabbi.
Rabbi Julia Neuberger

REMEMBER

I can't remember anybody's name. Why do you think the 'Dahling' thing started?
Eva Gabor, sister of Zsa Zsa

R E P U T A T I O N

Miss Frances Wright was known by name and
reputation to almost everyone. The outrageous nature
of her experimental colony and the scandals that had
come out of it had made her a general subject of gossip
. . . as a result, almost everyone planned to attend her
lectures, see her in person and be scandalised.
Fanny Trollope

I feel like I'm fighting a battle when I didn't start a war.
Dolly Parton

You make Al Capone look like a petty shoplifter.
Cynthia Israel, Shareholder in Burton Group Plc, complaining
about a plan to help chairman Ralph Halpern buy a mansion in
Hampstead, January 1982

Don't ever wear artistic jewellery; it wrecks a woman's
reputation.
Colette

When I appear in public people expect me to neigh,
grind my teeth, paw the ground and swish my tail –
none of which is easy.
Princess Anne

Until you have lost your reputation, you never realize
what a burden it was or what freedom really is.
Margaret Mitchell (1909-49), American novelist, Gone With the
Wind

Nobody's interested in sweetness and light.
Hedda Hopper (1890-1966), Hollywood gossip columnist

I used to be snow white but I drifted.
Mae West

During the month of June I acted as a pony express
rider carrying the American mail between Deadwood
and Custer, a distance of fifty miles . . . It was
considered the most dangerous route in the hills, but as
my reputation as a rider and quick shot was well
known, I was molested very little, for the toll gatherers
looked on me as being a good fellow, and they know
that I never missed my mark.
Calamity Jane

REVELATIONS

From the age of thirteen I had revelations from Our
Lord by a voice which told me how to behave.
Joan of Arc

REVOLUTION

If there's no dancing, count me out.
Emma Goldman *(1869-1940), American anarchist, commenting
on the Russian Revolution*

The traditional figures of revolution, Rousseau, Karl
Marx, Lenin and others, were no great emancipators of
women and were themselves chauvinists. They left their
wives slaving over a hot stove.
Sally Oppenheim*, British Conservative politician*

To be a revolutionary you have to be a human being.
You have to care about people who have no power.
Jane Fonda

Revolutionaries do not make revolutions. The
revolutionaries are those who know when power is
lying in the street and then they can pick it up. Armed
uprising by itself has never yet led to revolution.
Hannah Arendt *(1906-75), American political philosopher*

RIGHTS

The phrase 'Black is Beautiful' was invented by the
whites in South Africa to raise the morale of the black
people.
Mary Francis*, wife of writer Dick Francis*

You can be up to your boobies in white satin, with
gardenias in your hair and no sugar cane for miles, but
you can still be working on a plantation.
Billie Holiday

I do not ask for my rights. I have no rights. I have only
wrongs.
Caroline Norton *(1808-77), British poet and campaigner for
women's rights, when a court upheld her husband's refusal to
maintain her*

We are not ashamed of what we have done, because,
when you have a great cause to fight for, the moment of
greatest humiliation is the moment when the spirit is
proudest.
Emmeline Pankhurst (1858-1928), British suffragette

We have taken this action, because as women . . . we
realise that the condition of our sex is so deplorable that
it is our duty even to break the law in order to call
attention to the reasons why we do so.
Emmeline Pankhurst, speaking in court, October 1908

Women had always fought for men, and for their
children. Now they were ready to fight for their own
human rights. Our militant movement was established.
Emmeline Pankhurst

ROMANCE

Oh, what a dear ravishing thing is the beginning of an
amour!
Aphra Behn

You need someone to love you, while you're looking for
someone to love.
Shelagh Delaney, English writer

'Yes' I answered you last night;
'No,' this morning, Sir I say.
Colours seen by candlelight
will not look the same by day.
Elizabeth Barrett Browning

Romance, like the rabbit at the dog track, is the elusive,
fake, and never attained reward which, for the benefit
and amusement of our masters, keeps us running and
thinking in safe circles.
Beverly Jones, American feminist writer

That the man I worked for would fall in love and marry
me and he did. Ray was my team leader when I was
training to be an accountant. He had a blonde but
vapid girlfriend and I thought, he can do better than
that. I sent him an unsigned Valentine card and, when
he realised who it was from, we were on our way.
*Edwina Currie MP on being asked what is her most romantic
fantasy*

I am a romantic. Love affairs are the only real education in life.
Marlene Dietrich

ROYALTY

The King bathes, and with great success; a machine follows the Royal one into the sea, filled with fiddlers, who play God Save the King as his majesty takes his plunge.
Frances Burney D'Arblay (1752-1840), British novelist referring to King George III at Weymouth

SCOTLAND

If we were in Scotland, we could bring it in not proven. That's not guilty, but don't do it again.
Winifred Duke (1890-1962), English writer

SEASONS

Winter changes into stone the water of heaven and the heart of man.
Fantine in Victor Hugo's Les Miserables

Winter comes like an idiot, babbling and strewing flowers.
Edna St Vincent Millay

Winter is cold hearted,
Spring is yea and nay,
Autumn is a weather cock
Blown every way.
Summer days for me
When every leaf is on its tree.
Christina Rossetti

I only know that summer sang in me
A little while, that in me sings no more.
Edna St Vincent Millay

SECURITY

Security is when I'm very much in love with somebody extraordinary who loves me back.
Shelley Winters

Security is a mortal's chiefest enemy.
Ellen Terry

Well-adjusted people may get caught up in a tangle of social forces that makes them goose-step their way toward such abominations as the calculated execution of six million Jews ... It may be comforting to believe that the horrors of World War II were the work of a dozen or so insane men, but it is a dangerous belief, one that may give us a false sense of security.
Molly Harrower

SELF-KNOWLEDGE

We may fail of our happiness, strive we ever so bravely; but we are less likely to fail if we measure with judgement our chances and our capabilities.
Agnes Replier, The Spinster

When one is a stranger to oneself then one is estranged from others too.
Anne Morrow Lindbergh, Moon Shell

I need to take an emotion breath, step back, and remind myself who's actually in charge of my life.
Judith M. Knowlton

There's a period of life when we swallow a knowledge of ourselves and it becomes either good or sour inside.
Pearl Bailey

Men look at themselves in mirrors. Women look for themselves.
Elissa Melamed

You say I am mysterious
Let me explain myself
In a land of oranges
I am faithful to the apples
Elsa Gidlow

No one. I'm happy the way I am. God gave me what I
have, so I try to keep it in good order.
Edwina Currie MP, *on being asked who she would like to look
like*

My guru gave me one precept.
From without withdraw your gaze within
And fix it on the Inmost Self.
Taking to heart this one precept
Naked I began to roam.
Lal Ved, *fourteenth century*

I know I'm black, I see it all the time, I like it. I
wouldn't want to wash it off.
Joan Armatrading

Am I fact? Or am I fiction? Am I what I know I am? Or
am I what he thinks I am?
Angela Carter

I can throw a fit. I'm a master at it.
Madonna

Deep down I'm pretty superficial.
Ava Gardner

I'm a tuning fork, tense and twanging all the time.
Edna O'Brien

Pray, good people, be civil. I am the Protestant whore.
Nell Gwyn, *to a hostile crowd that mistook her for the Catholic
Duchess of Portland*

I always knew I was special. I always wanted to be a
star.
Anita Roddick

I wish I didn't look the way I do. I am a very pragmatic,
determined woman but my looks belie the way I am.
They make me look more frivolous, not a serious
thinker.
Pat Booth, *author*

I am painted as the greatest little dictator, which is
ridiculous – you always take some consultations.
Margaret Thatcher

Oh, I have lots of human weaknesses, who hasn't?
Margaret Thatcher

I'm not hard – I'm frightfully soft. But I will not be hounded.
Margaret Thatcher

Without self-confidence we are as babes in the cradle. And how can we generate this imponderable quality, which is yet so invaluable, most quickly? By thinking that other people are inferior to oneself. By feeling that one has some innate superiority – it may be wealth, or rank, a straight nose, or the portrait of a grandfather by Romney – for there is no end to the pathetic devices of the human imagination – over other people.
Virginia Woolf

I never rest easy and think, haven't I done well? I always think, oh God, I'm going to blow it!
Ruby Wax, *American entertainer*

The total understanding and realisation of my self might require eons for me to accomplish. But when that awareness is achieved, I will be aligned completely with that unseen divine force that we call God.
Shirley Maclaine, Dancing in the Light

I remembered a dream I used to have as a child – a rather prophetically sophisticated dream as I look back on it now. I dreamed I was being chased by a gorilla. I ran until I came to the edge of an abyss. Then I had a choice. I could confront the gorilla or jump, out of fear, into the abyss. I turned to the gorilla and said 'What do I do now?'
The gorilla threw up his hands and answered, 'I don't know, kid, it's your dream.'
That's just about how I look at things now. It's all my dream. I'm making all of it happen – good and bad – and I have the choice of how I'll relate to it and what I'll do about it.
Shirley Maclaine, It's All in the Playing

I'm a woman who has undoubtedly made a success of her career but not of her life. The myth of Bardot is finished, but Brigitte is me.
Brigitte Bardot, *on her fiftieth birthday, 1984*

I just think what a stupid sod I was – it got me into so much trouble.
Judith Ward *on her wrongful conviction for terrorism*

SELF-WORTH

God's gifts put man's best dreams to shame.
Elizabeth Barrett Browning

The recognition of self as valuable for being what it is
can be a strong basis for solidarity among the oppressed
whether black in a white society, female in a male-
dominated society or Muslim in a Hindu society.
Dvaki Jain

Don't compromise yourself. You're all you've got.
Janice Joplin

Women who set a low value on themselves make life
hard for all women.
Nellie McClung

Painting changed me. Instead of feeling a hopeless
muddle, inadequate in any given situation, doomed to
be a misfit, an urgent purpose gave me direction. Using
paint as a medium of transport, as it were, I had found
a way to cast out my inner confusion.
Nicolette Devas

The only way to enjoy anything in this life is to earn it
first.
Ginger Rogers, American film star

In overcoming seemingly insurmountable obstacles, I
learned that my oversized body wasn't the biggest
barrier to my self-esteem. To regain a healthy sense of
self-worth I first had to break down old fears, doubts
and anxieties. Only then was I able to reshape my
image successfully. Now my exterior and interior are in
harmony. I really feel as good as I look. And dammit, I
know I look good.
Elizabeth Taylor

No coward soul is mine
No trembler in the world's storm-troubled sphere;
I see heaven's glories shine,
And faith shines equal, arming me from fear.
Emily Brontë

I think it's one of the scars in our culture that we have
too high an opinion of ourselves. We align ourselves
with the angels instead of the higher primates.
Angela Carter, British writer

Most of our platitudes notwithstanding, self deception remains the most difficult deception. The tricks that work on others count for nothing in that very well-lit back alley where one keeps assignations with oneself: no winning smiles will do here, no prettily drawn lists of good intentions.
Joan Didion

It is terrible to destroy a person's picture of himself in the interests of truth or some other abstraction.
Doris Lessing

To have that sense of one's intrinsic worth which constitutes self-respect is potentially to have everything; the ability to discriminate, to love and to remain indifferent. To lack it is to be locked within oneself, paradoxically incapable of either love or indifference.
Joan Didion

My parents gave me considerable personal confidence. I am an only child and my parents always told me I could do anything in life and made me feel that I could talk to anybody. I also had a fairly forceful grandmother who was as undomesticated as I am. Sadly for her she was born into the wrong environment. She would have made a great suffragette.
Rabbi Julia Neuberger

Why not be oneself? That is the whole secret of a successful appearance. If one is a greyhound, why try to look like a Pekinese?
Edith Sitwell (1887-1964), *British poet and writer*, Why I Look as I Do, 1915

Speak up for yourself, or you'll end up a rug.
Mae West

I want people to appreciate me for who I am.
Julia Roberts

Some people are more courageous and get over it faster. But for women who married young and never worked, it is much harder. If they ask me I tell them to get a job – maybe just a small job. Or try to get on a typing course. Try to use whatever they are good at. It is tough. You can't allow yourself to pity yourself for too long.
Ivana Trump on divorce

S E N S E S

Nothing reaches the intellect before making its appearance in the senses.
Latin proverb

Make the most of every sense: glory in all the facets of pleasure and beauty which the world reveals to you through the several means of contact which nature provides. But of all the senses, sight must be the most delightful.
Helen Keller

S E X

The girl speaks eighteen languages and can't say no in any of them.
Dorothy Parker

To err is human – but it feels divine.
Mae West

If sex is such a natural phenomenon how come there are so many books on how to?
Bette Midler

I'm saving the bass player for Omaha.
Janis Joplin

After we made love he took a piece of chalk and made an outline of my body.
Joan Rivers

It doesn't matter what you do in the bedroom as long as you don't do it in the street and frighten the horses.
Mrs Patrick Campbell, British actress

Unless there is some emotional tie I'd rather play tennis.
Bianca Jagger

Except for the few years between the invention of the pill and the discovery of herpes, sex has always been dangerous.
Vogue *magazine*

She's the original good time that was had by all.
Bette Davis

For all the pseudo-sophistication of twentieth-century sex theory, it is still assumed that a man should make love as if his principal intention was to people the wilderness.
Germaine Greer

The more sex becomes a non-issue in people's lives, the happier they are.
Shirley Maclaine

I've tried several varieties of sex. The conventional position makes me claustrophobic and the others give me a stiff neck or lockjaw.
Tallulah Bankhead

The important thing in acting is to be able to laugh and cry. If I have to cry, I think of my sex life. If I have to laugh, I think of my sex life.
Glenda Jackson

My method is basically the same as Masters and Johnson, only they charge thousands of dollars and it's called therapy. I charge fifty dollars and it's called prostitution.
Xaviera Hollander, prostitute and writer

Men always fall for frigid women because they put on the best show.
Fanny Brice

There is no known way of increasing male sperm production.
Dr Virginia E. Johnson

When grown-ups do it it's kind of dirty – that's because there's no one to punish them.
Tuesday Weld

I didn't know how babies were made until I was pregnant with my fourth child five years later.
Loretta Lynn

I didn't get ahead by sleeping with people. Girls take heart!
Barbara Walters

Basically, heterosexuality means men first. That's what it's all about.
Charlotte Bunch

I've never been able to sleep with anyone. I require a full-size bed so that I can lie in the middle of it and extend my arms spread-eagle on both sides without being obstructed.
Mae West

I've only slept with the men I've been married to. How many women can make that claim?
Elizabeth Taylor

Personally, I like sex and I don't care what a man thinks of me as long as I get what I want from him – which is usually sex.
Valerie Perrine

I've never taken up with a congressman in my life . . . I've never gone below the Senate.
Barbara Howar

It is depressing to have to insist that sex is not an unnecessary, morally dubious self-indulgence but a basic human need, no less for women than for men.
Ellen Willis

The crusaders, we are told, put their wives into chastity belts before they sailed off for the Holy Land. They did not, for certain, put their own sexual equipment out of action for the duration.
Mary Stott

Ducking for apples – change one letter and it's the story of my life.
Dorothy Parker

Whatever else can be said about sex, it cannot be called a dignified performance.
Helen Lawrenson

Nature abhors a virgin – a frozen asset.
Clare Booth Luce

I shall not say why and how I became, at the age of fifteen, the mistress of the Earl of Craven.
Harriette Wilson, Memoirs

Women complain about sex more than men. Their gripes fall into two major categories: (1) Not enough; (2) Too much.
Ann Landers, American writer and journalist

The only reason I would take up jogging is so that I could hear heavy breathing again.
Erma Bombeck

An orgasm is just a reflex like a sneeze.
Dr Ruth (Westheimer)

In fact, it's quite ridiculous, the shapes people throw when they get down to it. There are few positions more ridiculous to look at than the positions people adopt when they are together. Limbs everywhere. Orifices gaping. Mucus pouring out and in. Sweat flying. Sheets wrecked. Animals and insects fleeing the scene when the going gets rough. Noise? My dear the evacuation of Dunkirk in World War Two was an intellectual discussion compared to it. Once in a while, of course, there's silence. Usually afterwards. It's called exhaustion.
Nell McCafferty

I like a man what takes his time.
Mae West

Some men are all right in their place – if they only knew the right places!
Mae West

In real life, women are always trying to mix something up with sex – religion, or babies, or hard cash; it is only men who long for sex separated out without rings or strings.
Katherine Whitehorn

I'd rather have a good bowl of soup.
Margaret Houston

All too many men still believe, in a rather naïve and egocentric way, that what feels good to them is automatically what feels good to women.
Shere Hite

I am happy now that Charles calls on my bed chamber less frequently than of old. As it is I now endure but two calls a week and when I hear his steps outside my door I lie down on my bed, close my eyes, open my legs and think of England.
Lady Alice Hillingdon, 1912

The truth is sex doesn't mean that much to me now.
Lana Turner

Oh, not at all – just a straight-away pounder.
Lillie Langtry, on being asked if the Prince of Wales was a romantic lover

As for the topsyturvy tangle known as *soixante-neuf* personally I have always felt it to be madly confusing, like trying to pat your head and rub your stomach at the same time.
Helen Lawrenson

Conventional sexual intercourse is like squirting jam into a doughnut.
Germaine Greer

My husband is a German: every night I get dressed up like Poland and he invades me.
Bette Midler

Most plain girls are virtuous because of the scarcity of the opportunity to be otherwise.
Maya Angelou

There will be sex after death – we just won't be able to feel it.
Lily Tomlin

I said ten years ago that in ten years time it would be smart to be a virgin. Now everyone is back to virgins again.
Barbara Cartland

I know it does make people happy but to me it is just like having a cup of tea.
Cynthia Payne, after her acquittal over the famous sex-for-luncheon-vouchers case, 1987

I wish I had as much in bed as I get in the newspapers.
Linda Ronstadt

I'd like to do a love scene with him just to see what all the yelling is about.
Shirley Maclaine on her brother Warren Beatty

I think I made his back feel better.
Marilyn Monroe, after a private meeting with John F. Kennedy

There are a lot more interesting things in life than sex –
like reading.
Jean Alexander, the actress who played Coronation Street's *Hilda
Ogden*

Believe me, I have to work up a lot of courage to write
sex scenes and I've made my mother promise not to
read them. I can discuss sex with any man, woman or
child in the world, but not with my mother.
Shirley Conran, on her book, Crimson

People have always found my sex life of interest, but I
can do without sex.
Pamella Bordes

Good sex is absolutely wonderful for you – much better
than jogging.
Jilly Cooper, writer

All the evidence I've seen says that sex before marriage
isn't a good idea. Women are born virgins and sex is
something that is added to them. They are not
incomplete without it.
*Victoria Gillick, who campaigned, unsuccessfully, to prevent girls
under sixteen being prescribed the Pill without their parents'
consent.*

You remember your first mountain in much the same
way you remember having your first sexual experience,
except that climbing doesn't make as much mess and
you don't cry for a week if Ben Nevis forgets to phone
next morning.
Muriel Gray, TV presenter, writer and climbing enthusiast, The
First Fifty

I think sex is dead anyway.
Elizabeth Taylor

Sex, unlike justice, should not be seen to be done.
Evelyn Laye, British actress and singer

In America sex is an obsession; in other parts of the
world it is a fact.
Marlene Dietrich

It is a silly question to ask a prostitute why she does it
. . . These are the highest paid 'professional' women in
America.
Gael Sheehy, American writer and social critic

Most of the time women want it more than men. I do.
Donna Ewin, *Page Three girl*

Girls are taught from childhood that any exhibition of sexual feeling is unwomanly and intolerable; they also learn from an early age that if a woman makes a mistake it is upon her and upon her alone that social punishment will descend.
Mary Scharlieb *(1845-1930), British gynaecological surgeon,* The Seven Ages of Woman

I do not believe that the normal man's sex needs are stronger than the normal woman's. The average man's undoubtedly are, owing to the utterly false repression of the woman's and the utterly unnatural stimulation of the man's which have been current for so long.
Marie Stopes *(1880-1958), British birth-control campaigner*

Sex is the Tabasco sauce which an adolescent national palate sprinkles on every course in the menu.
Mary Day Winn *(1888-1965), American writer,* Adam's Rib, *1931*

I have never felt a strong sense of possession about anyone. Generally when people start sleeping with one another and all the rest, it ruins things. If they insist on it, one lets them. We think 'Oh God if I don't let him then he won't come back'. But that doesn't mean we're all like that mad about it. No, we feel we have to, don't we?
Marlene Dietrich

Women are more open about this sort of entertainment than they were ten years ago. They are more at ease about sex and regard it as an equal activity. Many women enjoy sex in other contexts and want to explore it as far as possible. There is too much cosiness in a lot of women's magazines, and it's a bit insulting. We are aiming for a more independent daring woman.
Isabel Koprowski

Women are not interested in sex as a bodily function. I don't think they find pictures of naked men with limp penises attractive. They prefer their imagination to be stimulated by moving images and erotic literature.
Rachel Shattock, *deputy editor of* Cosmopolitan

A mutual and satisfied sexual act is of great benefit to the average woman, the magnetism of it is health-giving. When it is not desired on the part of the woman she has no response, it should not take place. This is an act of prostitution and is degrading to the woman's finer sensibility, all the marriage certificates on earth to the contrary notwithstanding.
Margaret Sanger, *(1883-1966), American nurse and writer*

SEXUALITY

Sex-appeal is fifty per cent what you've got and fifty per cent what people think you've got.
Sophia Loren

Being a sex symbol has to do with an attitude, not looks. Most men think it's looks, most women know otherwise.
Kathleen Turner

It's a flesh market – you won't find finer flesh anywhere.
Julia Morley, *British organiser of Miss World contests*

If a man doesn't look at me when I walk into a room, he's gay.
Kathleen Turner

When she raises her eyelids it's as if she were taking off all her clothes.
Colette

Being a sex symbol was rather like being a convict.
Raquel Welch

A sex symbol becomes a thing. I hate being a thing.
Marilyn Monroe

SIMILES

Like using a guillotine to cure dandruff.
Clare Boothe Luce

His voice was as intimate as the rustle of sheets.
Dorothy Parker

SINGING

I've been told that nobody sings the word 'hunger' like I do.
Billie Holiday (1915-59), American singer

Anybody singing the blues is in a deep pit yelling for help.
Mahalia Jackson (1911-72), American blues and gospel singer

I can't stand to sing the same song the same way two nights in succession. If you can, then it ain't music, it's close order drill, or exercise or yodelling or something, not music.
Billie Holiday

SOCIETY

Society in its full sense . . . is never an entity separable from the individuals who compose it.
Ruth Benedict

Our society, like all other historic civilisations, is a patriarchy. The fact is evident at once if one recalls that the military, industry, technology, universities, science, political office, and finance – in short every avenue of power within society, including the coercive force of the police, is entirely in male hands.
Kate Millet

You think intercourse is a private act; it's not, it's a social act. Men are sexually predatory in life; and women are sexually manipulative. When two individuals come together and leave their gender outside the bedroom door, then they make love. If they take it inside with them they do something else because society is in the room with them.

Andrea Dworkin, *American feminist writer and critic*

SORROW

Sorrow is so easy to express and yet so hard to tell.

Joni Mitchell, *singer*

SPINSTERS

When you're a spinster of forty,
you're reduced to considering bids
from husbands inclined to be naughty
and divorcees obsessed with their kids.

Wendy Cope, *poet*

SPORT

It's almost seventeen years since I was last hauled up a mountainside with a metal bar across my bum, two poles in one hand and my arm around the anorak of an unknown Austrian whose only English was 'bend ze knees' and 'open ze legs'. Seventeen blissful years with nary a thought of green sunblock, purple reflective goggles or navy blue knickers and not a knot in my stomach, in anticipation of hurtling off a glacier with sweat running down my long johns into my boot bindings.

Maureen Lipman, *actress and writer, on the subject of skiing*

STRESS

In times of great stress, such as a four-day vacation, the thin veneer of family life wears off almost at once, and we are revealed in our true personalities.

Shirley Jackson *(1920-69), American novelist*

SUCCESS

Integrity is so perishable in the summer months of success.
Vanessa Redgrave

If you're small, you better be a winner.
Billie Jean King

I've got two reasons for success and I'm standing on both of them.
Betty Grable

The penalty of success is to be bored by the people who used to snub you.
Nancy, Lady Astor (1879-1964)

To be successful, a woman has to be much better at her job than a man.
Golda Meir

Success has made failures of many men.
Cindy Adams

Success to me is having ten honeydew melons and eating only the top half of each.
Barbra Streisand

Success is counted sweetest by those who ne'er succeed.
Emily Dickinson, poet

The best thing that can come with success is the knowledge that it is nothing to long for.
Liv Ullmann

A lot of executives keep up the pretence of being solid community members when they are sleeping with their secretaries. Hef's honest. He isn't burdened by success.
Christie Hefner, chief executive of Playboy Enterprises, on her father

Great jokes and huge success are worth murdering for.
Ruby Wax

A woman who is loved always has success.
Vicki Baum (1888-1960), Austrian-born American writer

I don't think success is harmful, as so many people say. Rather, I believe it indispensable to talent, if for nothing else than to increase the talent.
Jeanne Moreau, French actress

SUFFERING

Although the world is full of suffering, it is full also of the overcoming of it.
Helen Keller, Optimism, *1903*

One does not love a place less for having suffered in it.
Jane Austen

SUICIDE

If you are of the opinion that the contemplation of suicide is sufficient evidence of a poetic nature, do not forget that actions speak louder than words.
Fran Lebowitz

Razors pain you;
rivers are damp;
acids stain you
and drugs cause a cramp;
guns aren't lawful;
nooses give;
gas smells awful;
you might as well live.
Dorothy Parker

Some rainy winter Sundays when there's a little boredom, you should always carry a gun. Not to shoot yourself, but to know exactly that you're always making a choice.
Lina Wertmuller, *Italian film director*

SURVIVAL

To keep a lamp burning we have to keep putting oil in it.
Mother Teresa

The love expressed between women is particular and powerful, because we have had to love in order to live: love has been our survival.
Audre Lord

Surviving means being born over and over.
Erica Jong

All women hustle. Women watch faces, voices, gesture, moods. The person who has to survive through cunning.
Marge Piercy

I survived because I was tougher than anybody else.
Bette Davis

I felt any extremes of emotion were a luxury I could not afford myself. I had to channel my mind into keeping myself together and keeping my personal dignity intact. It would have been lovely to cry, to yell, to scream. But I felt in order to survive as a person I had to talk and keep very calm.
Jennifer Guinness, *who was kidnapped for eight days by a gang of criminals in Ireland in 1986*

Nothing and no one can destroy the Chinese people. They are relentless survivors. They are the oldest civilised people on earth. Their civilisation passes through phases but its basic characteristics remain the same. They yield, they bend to the wind, but they never break.
Pearl Buck *(1892-1973), American novelist,* China, Past and Present

It was very easy to say leave, but where were we going? The airport was closed. There was hardly any petrol. One time we almost thought about it. There was a convoy that we could have joined if we had been willing to supply our own car, our own petrol and accept the fact that if we broke down on the way we were left behind. We said no, to hell with it, we'll take our chances and stay, so we did. Jackie always thought he was too old and too poor to be kidnapped.
Sunnie Mann, *wife of ex-hostage Jackie Mann, who was kidnapped and held hostage in Beirut*

TALENT

It seemed so effortless.
Baroness O'Cathain *to Dame Kiri Te Kanawa*

Everyone has talent. What is rare is the courage to follow the talent to the dark place where it leads.
Erica Jong

Remember, Ginger Rogers did everything Fred Astaire did, but she did it backwards *and* in high heels.
Faith Whittlesey

I believe talent is like electricity. We do not understand electricity. We use it. Electricity makes no judgement. You can plug into it, and light up a lamp, keep a heart pump going, light a cathedral, or you can electrocute a person with it ... I think talent is like that. I believe every person is born with a talent.
Maya Angelous

All our talents increase in the using, and every faculty both good and bad, strengthens by exercise.
Anne Brontë, The Tenant of Wildfell Hall

It takes people a long time to learn the difference between talent and genius, especially ambitious young men and women.
Louisa May Alcott, Little Women

A middling talent makes a more serene life.
Iris Murdoch

TELEVISION

Television has proved that people will look at anything rather than each other.
Ann Landers

I'm still fuming over the fact that they took *Inspector Morse* off last Wednesday for the wretched football. More than most women I'm completely inoculated against all sports – especially cricket.
Frances Edmonds, *writer and wife of former England cricketer Phil Edmonds*

Let's face it – there are no plain women on television.
Anna Ford, *BBC newscaster*

THEATRE

There are two kinds of directors in the theatre. Those who think they are God and those who are certain of it.
Rhetta Hughes

Acting is not being emotional, but being able to express emotion.
Kate Reid

Actresses don't have husbands, they have attendants.
Margaret Anglin

Glorious bouquets and storms of applause . . . these are the trimmings which every artist naturally enjoys. But to move an audience in such a role, to hear in the applause that unmistakable note which breaks through good theatre manners and comes from the heart, is to feel that you have won through to life itself. Such pleasure does not vanish with the fall of the curtain, but becomes part of one's own life.
Dame Alicia Markova, *British ballerina and President of the London Festival Ballet*

THOUGHT

I loved them because it was a joy to find thoughts one might have, beautifully expressed . . . by someone . . . wiser than oneself.
Marlene Dietrich

The fundamental fact about the Greek was that he had to use his mind. The ancient priests had said, 'Thus far and no further. We set the limits on thought.' The Greeks said, 'All things are to be examined and called into question. There are no limits on thought.'
Edith Hamilton

To know how to say what others only know how to think is what makes men poets or sages; and to dare to say what others only dare to think makes men martyrs or reformers – or both.
Elizabeth Charles (1828-96), British writer

T I M E

Every successful revolution puts on in time the robes of the tyrant it has deposed.
Barbara Tuchman (1912-89), American writer and editor

There is a time for work, and a time for love. That leaves no other time.
Coco Chanel

I've been on a calendar, but never on time.
Marilyn Monroe

T O L E R A N C E

Toleration . . . is the greatest gift of the mind, it requires the same effort of the brain that it takes to balance oneself on a bicycle.
Helen Keller

T R A N Q U I L L I T Y

You will find that deep place of silence right in your own room, your garden or even your bathtub.
Elizabeth Kubler Ross

Sorrow is tranquillity remembered in emotion.
Dorothy Parker

TRAVEL

Too often travel, instead of broadening the mind,
merely lengthens the conversation.
Elizabeth Drew

On a plane you can pick up more and better people
than on any other public conveyance since the
stagecoach.
Anita Loos

Travel is the most private of pleasures. There is no
greater bore than the travel bore. We do not in the least
want to hear what he has seen in Hong Kong.
Vita Sackville-West, British writer

Travelling is the ruin of all happiness! There's no
looking at a building here after seeing Italy.
Fanny Burney

TRUST

I trusted him because of his family, and because he had
been to Eton.
Gwendoline Lamb, an investor who lost money when Justin
Frewen's company, Imperial Commodities, crashed in 1983

I find being faithful frightfully exciting, it makes
everything so much more interesting. You can open
yourself up to somebody through fidelity. There's trust,
you can be more brave about talking more openly and
it carries on into your physical life as well. Sharing a life
with somebody you trust is very vivid. If you're both
drifting away, interested in other people, it's all
diffused.
Jean Marsh, British actress

TRUTH

I don't care what is written about me so long as it isn't
true.
Dorothy Parker

Cynicism is an unpleasant way of saying the truth.
Lillian Hellman

The tombstone is about the only thing that can stand
upright and lie on its face at the same time.
Mary Wilson Little

Tell the truth
But let it slant.
Emily Dickinson

If truth is beauty, how come no one has their hair done
in the library?
Lily Tomlin, American comedy actress

Truth is so rare it's delightful to tell it.
Emily Dickinson

I never know how much of what I say is true.
Bette Midler

Just how difficult it is to write a biography can be
reckoned by anybody who sits down and considers just
how many people know the real truth about his or her
love affairs.
Rebecca West

I think if the people of this country can be reached with
the truth, their judgment will be in favour of the many,
as against the privileged few.
Eleanor Roosevelt (1884-1962), in the Ladies' Home Journal

Nobody speaks the truth when there's something they
must have.
Elizabeth Bowen (1899-1973), Irish novelist, The House of Paris

Nagging is the repetition of unpalatable truths.
Lady Edith Summerskill (1901-80), British Labour politician

When a subject is highly controversial . . . one cannot
hope to tell the truth. One can only show how one
came to hold whatever opinion one does hold. One can
only give one's audience the chance of drawing their
own conclusions as they observe the limitations, the
prejudices, the idiosyncrasies of the speaker.
Virginia Woolf

It's very difficult to get over to people what his strengths
are, his leadership qualities, his sense of humour, his
gentle, more sensitive side. I sometimes can't believe the
distortion of the truth.
Glenys Kinnock, on her husband

VALUES

I'd rather have roses on my table than diamonds on my neck.
Emma Goldman *(1869-1940), American anarchist*

Ninety-nine per cent of what we say is about values. I firmly believe that ethical capitalism is the best way of changing society for the better.
Anita Roddick

Victorian values ... were the values when our country became great.
Margaret Thatcher

VIOLENCE

Non-violence is a flop. The only bigger flop is violence.
Joan Baez, *American singer*

In violence we forget who we are.
Mary McCarthy

VIRTUE

Virtue has its own reward, but no sale at the box-office.
Mae West

A wife is sought for her virtue, a concubine for her beauty.
Chinese proverb

WAR

If we justify war it is because all peoples always justify the traits of which they find themselves possessed.
Ruth Benedict

Today, the real test for power is not capacity to make war but capacity to prevent it.
Anne O'Hare McCormick

Dead battles, like dead generals, hold the military mind in their dead grip.
Barbara Tuchman

I could not give my name to aid slaughter in this war, fought on both sides for grossly material ends, which did not justify the sacrifice of a single mother's son. Clearly, I must continue to oppose it, and expose it, to all whom I could reach with my voice or pen.
Sylvia Pankhurst (1882-1960), British suffragette

Be the Emperor, be Peter the Great, John the Terrible, the Emperor Paul – crush them all under you – now don't you laugh, naughty one – but I long to see you so with those men who try to govern you and it must be the contrary.
Empress Alexandra, Consort to Russia (1872-1918), in a letter to Tsar Nicholas II, 1916

Everything, everything in war is barbaric . . . but the worst barbarity of war is that it forces men collectively to commit acts against which individually they would revolt with their whole being.
Ellen Key, War, Peace and the Future

I have gone to war too . . . I am going to fight capitalism even if it kills me. It is wrong that people like you should be comfortable and well fed while all around you people are starving.
Sylvia Pankhurst

In this House, we are not interested in the possibilities of defeat, they do not exist.
Queen Victoria referring to the Boer War

Militarism . . . is one of the chief bulwarks of capitalism, and the day that militarism is undermined, capitalism will fail.
Helen Keller (1880-1968), American writer and lecturer, The Story of My Life

Après nous le deluge (After us the deluge).
Madame de Pompadour (1721-64), mistress of Louis XV of France, after the Battle of Rossbach, 1757

War is a thing of fearful and curious anomalies . . . It has shown that government by men only is not an appeal to reason, but an appeal to arms, that on women, without a voice to protest, must fall the burden. It is easier to die than to send a son to death.
Mary Roberts Rinehard (1876-1958)

Russia still writhed and stumbled. The wave of revolts and uprisings, the constant agitations, the incessant inflammatory orations of men possessed of little political competence had by this time cowed the emperor and the ruling class into bewildered and sullen inertia.
Grand Duchess Maria of Russia *(1890-1958), referring to the Russian Revolution of 1917*

WILL POWER

The only way to stop smoking is to just stop – no ifs, ands or butts.
Edith Zittler

Nature has a funny way of sending us what we most resist. None of us can remain smugly immune from addiction, whether it is chocolate, cigarettes, alcohol, drugs, or even work. Many will use these addictive 'tools' to distract them from having to face life in a changing and testing world.
Princess Diana

WISDOM

Do not insult the mother alligator until after you have crossed the river.
Haitian proverb

Logic is in the eye of the logician.
Gloria Steinem

To understand everything makes one very indulgent.
Madame de Staël

WIT

Don't be humble. You're not that great.
Golda Meir

Henry James chews more than he bites off.
Mrs Henry Adams, c. 1880

Wit lies in the likeness of things that are different, and in the difference of things that are alike.
Madame de Staël

It is possible that blondes also prefer gentlemen.
Mamie Van Doren, American film actress

A camel looks like a horse that was planned by a committee.
Vogue *magazine, July 1958*

There's a helluva distance between wisecracking and wit. Wit has truth in it; wisecracking is simply callisthenics with words.
Dorothy Parker

Wit in a woman is apt to have bad consequences; like a sword without a scabbard, it wounds the wearer and provokes assailants. I am sorry to say the generality of women who have excelled in wit have failed in chastity.
Elizabeth Montagu (1720-1800)

WOMAN

I'm just a person trapped inside a woman's body.
Elaine Boosler (1858-1950)

Our [women's] bodies are shaped to bear children and our lives are a worship out of the processes of creation. All ambition and intelligence are beside that great elemental point.
Phyllis McGinley, The Honour of Being a Woman

A woman is a woman until the day she dies, but a man's a man only as long as he can.
Moms Mabley

Yes, I am wise, but it's wisdom full of pain
Yes, I've paid the price, but look how much I've gained.
I am wise, I am invincible, I am woman.
Helen Reddy, singer

One is not born a woman, but rather becomes a woman.
Simone de Beauvoir

How much bondage and suffering a woman escapes when she takes the liberty of being her own physician of both body and soul.
Elizabeth Cady Stanton

I think that women have it made if they know how to go about it. A woman don't have to work really if she don't want to and if she is smart enough to make a man a good wife he's gonna take care of her.
Dolly Parton

I have bursts of being a lady, but it doesn't last long. I'm the modern intelligent independent type woman. In other words, a girl who can't get a man.
Shelley Winters

Being a woman is of special interest only to aspiring male transsexuals. To actual women, it is simply a good excuse not to play football.
Fran Lebowitz

The great and almost only comfort about being a woman is that one can always pretend to be more stupid than one is and no one is surprised.
Freya Stark, American writer

I should like to know what is the proper function of women, if it is not to make reasons for husbands to stay at home, and still stronger reasons for bachelors to go out.
George Eliot

There are two kinds of women: those who want power in the world, and those who want power in bed.
Jacqueline Kennedy Onassis

Behind almost every woman you ever heard of stands a man who let her down.
Naomi Bliven, American writer

And the crazy part of it was even if you were clever, even if you spent your adolescence reading John Donne and Shaw, even if you studied history or zoology or physics and hoped to spend your life pursuing some difficult and challenging career you still had a mind full of all the soupy longings that every high school girl was awash in . . . underneath it all you longed to be annihilated by love, to be swept off your feet, to be filled up by a giant prick spouting sperm, soapsuds, silk and satins, and, of course, money.
Erica Jong

A woman can look both moral and exciting . . . If she
also looks as if it was quite a struggle.
Edna Ferber *(1887-1968), American writer*

Both women and melons are best when fairly ripe.
Spanish proverb

If you take a woman fishing, it has to be a dull one.
Anybody lively scares away the fish. There's a special
type of woman, in fact, who is chosen for fishing
holidays.
Elizabeth Jenkins *(1862-1933)*

You don't know a woman until you have had a letter
from her.
Ada Leverson *(1862-1933), English writer*

In nine cases out of ten, a woman had better show more
affection than she feels.
Jane Austen

Some women like to sit down with trouble as if it were
knitting.
Ellen Glasgow *(1873-1945), American novelist*

I love being a woman. You can cry. You get to wear
pants now. If you're on a boat and it's going to sink,
you get to go on the rescue boat first. You get to wear
cute clothes. It must be a great thing, or so many men
wouldn't be wanting to do it.
Gilda Radner

We have no faith in ourselves. I have never met a
woman who, deep down in her core, really believes she
has great legs. And if she suspects that she might have
great legs, then she's convinced that she has a shrill
voice and no neck.
Cynthia Heimel, *author of* If You Can't Live Without Me, Why
Aren't You Dead Yet?

A homely face and no figure have aided many women
heavenward.
Minna Antrim, *American writer*, Naked Truth

It's nothing to be born ugly, sensibly the ugly woman
comes to terms with her ugliness and exploits it as a
grace of nature.
Colette, Journey for Myself

Had I been a man I might have explored the poles or climbed Mount Everest, but as it was my spirit found outlet in the air.
Amy Johnson (1903-41), British pilot, Myself When Young

A woman, especially if she have the misfortune of knowing anything, should conceal it as well she can.
Jane Austen, Northanger Abbey

Women never have young minds. They are born three thousand years old.
Shelagh Delaney, British dramatist, A Taste of Honey

I would venture to guess that Anon, who wrote so many poems without signing them, was often a woman.
Virginia Woolf, The Moment and Other Essays

Intimacies between women often go backwards, beginning in revelations and ending in small talk without loss of esteem.
Elizabeth Bowen (1899-1973), Irish novelist, The Death of the Heart

Publicity in women is detestable. Anonymity runs in their blood. The desire to be veiled still possesses them. They are not even now as concerned about the health of their fame as men are, and, speaking generally, will pass a tombstone or a signpost without feeling an irresistible desire to cut their names on it.
Virginia Woolf

I believe it is incredibly important for women to support other women so that in time success and achievement are not remarkable by gender.
Brenda Dean, General Secretary, SOGAT

Women give themselves to God when the Devil wants nothing more to do with them.
Sophie Arnould (1740-1802), French operatic soprano

A woman is like a teabag – only when in hot water do you realise how strong she is.
Nancy Reagan

Good women always think that it is their fault when someone else is being offensive. Bad women never take the blame for anything.
Anita Brookner, British writer

She is clearly the best man among them.
Barbara Castle, British politician, on Margaret Thatcher

She was a gentlewoman, a scholar and a saint, and after having been three times married she took the vow of celibacy. What more could be expected of any woman?
Elizabeth Wordsworth

Women live like bats or owls, labour like beasts, and die like worms.
Margaret Cavendish (1623-73) Duchess of Newcastle, English writer

If ever there was a colonised race on this planet it's the female race, there's no question about that.
Shirley Maclaine

Every young woman in our land should be qualified by some accomplishment which she may teach, or some art or profession she can follow, to support her credibility, should the necessity occur.
Sarah Josepha Hale

Miss Brodie said: ' Pavlova contemplates her swans in order to perfect her swan dance, she studies them. This is true dedication. You must all grow up to be dedicated women as I have dedicated myself to you.'
Muriel Spark, The Prime of Miss Jean Brodie

Total commitment to family and total commitment to career is possible, but fatiguing.
Muriel Fox, American business executive and feminist

I was the first woman to run a film festival: not only that but I was quite young as well, so it's rather interesting that they let me get away with it. We basically showed every movie we could find by a woman director. We found that Ida Lupino was the only woman director working in Hollywood in the 1950s. Obviously there were women directors before her – there's a whole tradition, people like Dorothy Arzner in the 1930s – but somehow Lupino appeals to me more – she has a more feminine approach. That's what I like about her; she was quintessentially her own woman.
Lynda Myles, Senior Vice-President of Creative Affairs Europe, Columbia Pictures

In mid-life today – those years from about mid-thirties to mid-fifties – a new kind of woman is emerging. No longer is she expected to marry, run her home, rear her children till the last in the nest has flown, and then pick up the pieces as best she can, perhaps finding a job, perhaps sliding into a passive and not always rewarding middle age. Today this woman has the opportunity to be in the prime of her life.
Helen Franks, Prime Time

Superwoman is perfection as a wife, her house is always spotless, her husband's shirts laundered at home, 'because the laundry do them so badly'. Although she does a full-time job, she is able to give intimate little dinners for her husband's business clients once or twice a week, type out his reports, watch his calorie intake, rev up in gold lamé every night in bed, yet be up to cook his breakfast, and hand him his briefcase and umbrella as he sets out for work. All her girlfriends detest her.
Jilly Cooper

I know I have the body of a weak and feeble woman, but I have the heart and stomach of a king, and of a king of England too.
Queen Elizabeth I, *in a speech at Tilbury on the approach of the Spanish Armada*

A woman cuts her wisdom teeth when she is dead.
Proverb

Women have long hair and short brains.
Proverb

The vote, I thought, means nothing to women. We should be armed.
Erica Jong, *epigraph to* Fear of Flying,

Over one thousand women have gone to prison in the course of this agitation, have suffered their imprisonment, have come out of prison injured in health, weakened in body, but not in spirit.
Emmeline Pankhurst

The keeping of an idle woman is a badge of superior social status.
Dorothy L. Sayers

You may marry or you may not. In today's world that
is no longer the big question for women. Those who
grab on to men so that they can collapse with relief,
spend the rest of their days shining up their status
symbols and figures. They never have to reach, stretch,
learn, grow, face dragons or make a living again are the
ones to be pitied. They, in my opinion, are the
unfulfilled ones.
Helen Gurley Brown, *American writer,* Sex and the Single Girl,
1963

Under the umbrella of NAWO we have all kinds of
women coming together because they recognise that
there is a woman's common ground. There are young
women who may be interested in their own
advancement, but that doesn't mean they don't have
any solidarity with other women.
Jane Grant, *British Director of the National Alliance of Women's
Organisations, 1991*

Female size, especially brain size, has always been held
to explain their unfitness for this or that; whole
nineteenth-century theories were based on the smaller
size of the brain of women and 'inferior races' – until it
was found that elephants' brains were even larger than
men's.
Katherine Whitehorn, *British journalist*

But now it is not as a woman descending from noble
ancestry, but as one of the people that I am avenging
lost freedom, my scourged body, the outraged chastity
of my daughters. Roman lust has gone so far that not
our very persons, not even age or virginity, are left
unpopulated . . . This is a woman's resolve; as for men,
they may live and be slaves.
Boadicea, Queen of the Iceni *(native Britons) during the first
century* AD

Civilised woman can't do the right thing without paying
too high a price.
Margaret Drabble, *British writer,* The Middle Ground

But after all, I'm a woman. A woman can't play as a
man plays. She hasn't the physique and energy. A
woman's hand is a limitation in itself.
Jacqueline du Pré *(1945-87), British cellist*

A fair woman is a paradise to the eye, a purgatory to
the purse, and a hell to the soul.
Elizabeth Grymeston (1563-1603), English writer

W H A T   W O M E N   W A N T

Women want men, careers, money, children, friends,
luxury, comfort, independence, freedom, respect, love
and a three-dollar pantihose that won't run.
Phyllis Diller

What this woman wants, with all due respect to
Sigmund Freud, is for men to stop asking that question
and to realise that women are human beings, not some
alien species. They want the same things men want.
Diane White

Women want family life that glitters and is stable. They
don't want some lump spouse watching ice hockey in
the late hours of his eighteenth beer. They want a family
that is so much fun and is so smart that they look
forward to Thanksgiving rather than regarding it with a
shudder. That's the glitter part. The stable part is,
obviously, they don't want to be one bead on a long
necklace of wives. They want, just like men, fun, love,
fame, money and power, and equal pay for equal work.
Carolyn See

Exactly what men want: love, money, excitement,
pleasure, happiness, fulfilling work – and sometimes a
child who will say 'I love you'.
Joyce Brothers

Freedom from pain, security, creature comforts and an
end to loneliness. When you get down to the basics, it's
still the same old story, a fight for love and glory.
Alice Kahn

Any idiot would know women's needs are simple. All
we want is your basic millionaire/brain surgeon/
criminal lawyer/great dancer who pilots his own Lear
jet and owns oceanfront property. On the other hand,
things being what they are today, most of us will settle
for a guy who holds down a steady job and isn't
carrying an infectious disease.
Linda Sunshine

I'd like to own Texas and lease Colorado.
Rita Mae Brown

W O M A N H O O D

Womanhood is the great fact in her life; wifehood and
motherhood are but incidental relations.
*Elizabeth Cady Stanton (1815-1902), American feminist and
suffragette*

W O M A N P O W E R

Women can save civilisation only by the broadest co-
operative action, by daring to think, by daring to be
themselves.
Harriet Stanton Blatch

W O M E N   A N D   M E N

A romantic man often feels more uplifted with two
women than with one; his love seems to hit the ideal
mark somewhere between the two different faces.
Elizabeth Bowen

Woman's life must be wrapped up in a man, and the
cleverest woman on earth is the biggest fool with a
man.
Dorothy Parker

Women are not men's equals in anything except
responsibility. We are not their inferiors, either, or even
their superiors. We are quite simply different races.
Phyllis McGinley

Women prefer men who have something tender about
them – especially the legal kind.
Kay Ingram

I don't mind living in a man's world as long as I can be
a woman in it.
Marilyn Monroe

A woman has to be twice as good as a man to go half as
far.
Fannie Hurst

Whether women are better than men I cannot say – but I can say they are certainly no worse.
Golda Meir

The king has been very good to me. He promoted me from a simple maid to be a marchioness. Then he raised me to be a queen. Now he will raise me to be a martyr.
Anne Boleyn

A man thinks he knows, but a woman knows better.
Chinese proverb

Men have been trained and conditioned by women, not unlike the way Pavlov conditioned his dogs, into becoming their slaves. As a compensation for their labours men are given periodic use of women's vaginas.
Esther Vilar

Plain women know more about men than beautiful ones do.
Katherine Hepburn

Woman serves as a looking-glass possessing the magic powers of reflecting the figure of man at twice its natural size.
Virginia Woolf

It is very Victorian of the council to think that the ladies of Darlington will lose control at the sight of a few male bodies.
Rita Fishwick, Mayor of Darlington, on a decision to ban a male strip show

A man who is honest with himself wants a woman to be soft and feminine, careful of what she's saying and talk like a man.
Ann-Margret, American film star

As I look around the West End these days, it seems to me that outside every thin girl is a fat man, trying to get in.
Katherine Whitehorn

Once you know what women are like, men get kind of boring. I'm not trying to put them down, I mean I like them sometimes as people, but sexually they're dull.
Rita Mae Brown, American novelist, Rubyfruit Jungle

If it's a woman, it's caustic; if it's a man, it's
authoritative.
Barbara Walters

Women are one of the Almighty's enigmas to prove to
men that he knows more than they do.
Ellen Glasgow

I'm not denyin' that women are foolish: God Almighty
made 'em to match the men.
George Eliot

Vain man is apt to think we were merely intended for
the world's propagation and to keep its human
inhabitants sweet and clean; but, by their leaves, had we
the same literature he would find our brains as fruitful
as our bodies.
Hannah Woolley, Gentlewoman's Companion, 1675

Girls are so queer you never know what they mean.
They say no when they mean yes, and drive a man out
of his wits for the fun of it.
Louisa May Alcott, Little Women

Women have always been the guardians of Wisdom
and Humanity which makes them natural, but usually
secret rulers. The time has come for them to rule
openly, but together with and not against men.
Dr Charlotte Wolff, *German-born British writer*, Bisexuality: A
Study

It makes me feel masculine to tell you that I do not
answer questions like this without being paid for
answering them.
Lillian Hellman (1905-84), *American dramatist, on being asked
by* Harper's *magazine when she felt most masculine. (This question
had already been asked of several famous men.)*

Sometimes I think if there was a third sex men
wouldn't get so much as a glance from me.
Amanda Vail (1921-66), *American writer*

Now one of the great reasons why so many husbands
and wives make shipwreck of their lives together is
because a man is always seeking for happiness while a
woman is still on a perpetual hunt for trouble.
Dorothy Dix (1861-1951), *American journalist and writer*

There's something about the rock 'n' roll tribe when it gets together that is really quite ludicrous to me. The men, they love it – they're like pigs in shit. When they start doing the lads' thing, I just have to go to my room.
Annie Lennox on being a woman in the music business

Every time a woman makes herself laugh at her husband's often told jokes she betrays him. The man who looks at his woman and says 'What would I do without you?' is already destroyed.
Germaine Greer

With men he can be rational and unaffected, but when he has ladies to please, every feature works.
Jane Austen

To be sure he's a man the male must see to it that the female be clearly a woman, the opposite of a 'man', that is, the female must act like a faggot.
Valerie Solanas, American artist and writer

I feel sorry for men – they have more problems than women. In the first place they have to compete with women.
Françoise Sagan, French novelist

I do not think women understand how repelled a man feels when he sees a woman wholly absorbed in what she is thinking, unless it is her child, or her husband, or her lover. It gives one gooseflesh.
Rebecca West

More and more it appears that, biologically, men are designed for short brutal lives and women for long and miserable ones.
Dr Estelle Ramey, *physiology professor, Georgetown University, 1985*

To be happy with a man you must understand him a lot and love him a little. To be happy with a woman you must love her a lot and not try to understand her at all.
Helen Rowland

Women are told from their infancy and taught by example of their mothers, that a little knowledge of human weakness, justly termed cunning, softness of temper, 'outward' obedience and a scrupulous attention to a puerile kind of propriety, will obtain for them the protection of man.
Mary Wollstonecraft

The only way for a woman to provide for herself decently is for her to be good to some man that can afford to be good to her.
Mrs Warren, Mrs Warren's Profession

There is nothing women hate so much as to see men selfishly enjoying themselves without the solace of feminine society.
Katherine Tynan Hinkson (1861-1931), *Irish poet and novelist*

When women go wrong, men go right after them.
Mae West

When you are born they tell you, 'what a pity that you are so clever, so intelligent, so beautiful but you are not a man', you are ashamed of your condition as a woman. I wanted to act like a man because the man was master.
Melina Mercouri, *Greek actress and political activist*

My mother said it was simple to keep a man, you must be a maid in the living room, a cook in the kitchen and a whore in the bedroom. I said I'd hire the other two and take care of the bedroom bit.
Jerry Hall, *American model and actress*

Fool! Don't you see now that I could have poisoned you a hundred times had I been able to live without you!
Cleopatra to Mark Antony

In the future people will believe from watching TV archives of the late twentieth century that men made up most of the population and most women had a life expectancy of only forty.
Jill Gascoigne, English actress

Oh daddy, buy me *that*.
Marlene Dietrich to her director on spotting John Wayne in the Universal Studios canteen

Once a woman has forgiven her man, she must not reheat his sins for breakfast.
Marlene Dietrich

Any woman who lets a man walk over her is a dumb idiot and deserves no better.
Edith Piaf (1915-63), French singer and cabaret artist

A woman fit to be a man's wife is too good to be his servant.
Dorothy Leigh, English author, The Mother's Blessing

Women get more unhappy the more they try to liberate themselves and act like men. A woman is a tender and sweet person and she'll lose that if she tries to be like a man.
Brigitte Bardot

Men they may have many faults
But women only two
Everything they say
And everything they do.
Anon

How can a man accuse a woman of nagging? If he had done what was asked of him in the first place, it would never need to be repeated. Therefore there would be no such thing as a nagging woman.
Kris Julin-Lawrence

WORDS

Sticks and stones are bad on bones
Aimed at angry art
Words can sting like anything
But silence breaks the heart.
Phyllis McGinley, Ballad of Lost Objects

The words the happy say are paltry melody. But those the silent feel are beautiful.
Emily Dickinson

A word after a word after a word is power.
Margaret Atwood

Language is magic – it makes things appear and disappear.
Nicole Brossard

We might have been – these are but common words and yet they make the sum of life's bewailing.
Letitia Landon (1802-38), *British poet and novelist*

One has to secrete a jelly in which to slip quotations down people's throats and one always secretes too much jelly.
Virginia Woolf

Blessed is the man, who having nothing to say, abstains from giving wordy evidence of the fact.
George Eliot

WORK

I don't feel any pressure or great responsibility because I love my work. I do my best and I am a success so it's fun and that makes all the difference. Today's models take the business very seriously, or a least some do. We work hard and often have two or three different things we're involved with. Models used to only have to look good, but today it's different.
Claudia Schiffer, supermodel

If I could always work in silence and obscurity, and let my efforts be known by their results.
Emily Brontë

I want to work for a company that contributes to and is part of the community. I want something not just to invest in. I want something to believe in.
Anita Roddick

Work is more fun than fun.
Anita Roddick

If there is a God and an after-life, I'll have the opportunity to do the same work up there.
Christie Hefner

I've never worked because of the money. Ask any pop singer – it's for the fame.
Cilla Black

I get to be with somebody I love, all day, every day.
Judy Finnigan, on being asked what is the best thing about her job. She presents This Morning, *with her husband Richard Madeley*

I felt that someone else could do the job far better than I.
Edwina Currie MP, after refusing a job in John Major's government, 1992

You can run an office without a boss, but you can't run an office without secretaries.
Jane Fonda

Work is the province of cattle.
Dorothy Parker

I'm not paranoid about my work. If they gave me up tomorrow I'd be upset and bruised, but I'd soon get over it because there are so many other things I want to do. I quite fancy being an antiques dealer, trundling round the country looking for bargains.
Gloria Hunniford, BBC presenter

He did leave here to do some work and he's away again now in Los Angeles recording, but Mick is always travelling. He's a workaholic.
Jerry Hall, on Mick Jagger

That is absolutely typical. He is incredibly brave and his job is everything to him.
Carol Barnes, TV newscaster, hearing that her cameraman husband was wounded while filming at Kabul Airport

No wonder I am so keen on Florence Nightingale, she just worked all the time for her whole life. There is something to be said for that once you have discovered a cause.
Laura Ashley (1925-85)

WORLD

So many gods, so many creeds,
So many paths that wind and wind.
While just the art of being kind
is all the sad world needs.
Ella Wheeler Wilcox *(1850-1919), American poet,* The World's
Need

Laugh and the world laughs with you;
Weep, and you weep alone,
for the sad old earth must borrow its mirth,
but has trouble enough of its own.
Ella Wheeler Wilcox, Solitude

Set the foot down with distrust on the crust of the
world – it is thin.
Edna St Vincent Millay, *American poet*

The Third World is not a reality but an ideology.
Hannah Arendt

WRITING

I've always believed in writing without a collaborator,
because where two people are writing the same book
each believes he gets all the worries and only half the
royalties.
Agatha Christie

If you're going to write, don't pretend to write down.
It's going to be the best you can do, and it's the best you
can do that kills you.
Dorothy Parker

Nothing you write, if you hope to be good, will ever
come out as you first hoped.
Lillian Hellman

I could write a whole book at one sitting if only I
didn't have to eat or sleep.
Enid Blyton *(1897-1968)*

I'm a lousy writer; a helluva lot of people have lousy
taste.
Grace Metalious, *author of* Peyton Place

Ball points belong to their age. They make everyone write alike.
Loraine Hansberry (1930-65), American playwright, in her diary of 1963

Walter Scott has no business to write novels, especially good ones. It is not fair. He has fame and profit enough as a poet, and should not be taking the bread out of other people's mouths. I do not like him, and do not mean to like *Waverley* if I can help it . . . But fear I must.
Jane Austen, writing to Anna Austen, 1814

Novelists should never allow themselves to weary of the study of real life.
Charlotte Brontë, The Professor

I've made characters live, so that people talk about them at cocktail parties, and that, to me, is what counts.
Jacqueline Susann, author of Valley of the Dolls

Once the grammar has been learned, writing is simply talking on paper and in time learning what not to say.
Beryl Bainbridge

Writers should be read, but neither seen nor heard.
Daphne du Maurier

The Poet speaks to all men of that other life of theirs that they have smothered and forgotten.
Edith Sitwell, Rhyme and Reason

I enjoyed talking to her, but I thought nothing of her writing. I considered her 'A beautiful little knitter'.
Edith Sitwell referring to Virginia Woolf, in a letter to G. Singleton

The idea that it is necessary to go to a university in order to become a successful writer, or even a man or a woman of letters (which is by no means the same thing) is one of those fantasies that surround authorship.
Vera Brittain (1893-1970), British writer and feminist

Writing is something I can carry on with until I die. It gives me far more pleasure than being a famous movie star.
Emma Thompson, British actress

All those writers who write about their childhood!
Gentle God, if I wrote about mine you wouldn't sit in
the same room with me.
Dorothy Parker

A woman must have money and a room of her own if
she is to write fiction.
Virginia Woolf

The paragraph is a great art form. I'm very interested in
paragraphs and I write paragraphs very, very carefully.
Iris Murdoch

Some collaboration has to take place in the mind
between the woman and the man before the act of
creation can be accomplished. Some marriage of
opposites has to be consummated. The whole of the
mind must lie wide open if we are to get the sense that
the writer is communicating his experience with perfect
fullness.
Virginia Woolf

Trivial personalities decomposing in the eternity of
print.
Virginia Woolf

I write two pages of arrant nonsense, after straining; I
write variations of every sentence; compromise; bad
shots; possibilities; till my writing book is like a
lunatic's dream.
Virginia Woolf

Not inspiration, practice.
Rebecca Harding Davis

A strange, horrible business, but I suppose good enough
for Shakespeare's day.
Queen Victoria, *giving her opinion of* King Lear

I have a Fleet Street training, the best in the world, so I
can't be a bad writer, can I?
Shirley Conran

YOUTH

Youth condemns: maturity condones.
Amy Lovell

How absurd and delicious it is to be in love with someone younger than yourself. Everyone should try it.
Barbara Pym, British writer

Paradoxical as it may seem, to believe in youth is to look backward: to look forward we must believe in age.
Dorothy Parker

For the very first time the young are seeing history being made before it is censored by their elders.
Margaret Mead

Young people ought not to be idle. It is very bad for them.
Margaret Thatcher

Youth is something very new; twenty years ago no one mentioned it.
Coco Chanel

It is often said that New York is a city for only the very rich and the very poor. It is less often said that New York is also, at least for those of us who came there from somewhere else, a city for only the very young.
Joan Didion

There is nothing can pay one for that invaluable ignorance which is the companion of youth; those sanguine groundless hopes and that lively vanity, which make all the happiness of life.
Lady Mary Wortley Montagu

A Final Word

When compiling the last few quotes and running the final spelling check, the computer's dictionary stumbled over many mistakes. However, it was interesting to note that it did not recognise two words, whose spelling was definitely correct: Womanpower and Childcare. After all this effort and with so much inspiration from the quotes I didn't know whether to laugh or cry. Yes, women have come a long way, but the journey is nowhere near over. Needless to say, these words were promptly added to the dictionary . . .

Alison Payne

INDEX